Sheet Pan Cookbook

By

Aron Smith

Dedication

One last toast to the time consuming, exhausting and utterly messy cooking methods that we shall see no more.

Table Of Contents

Introduction

Hello to you lovelies! I feel super excited. Don't you? Today is world sheet pan day! Well, not exactly, but I'm dedicating this entire book to the sheet pan. First of all its name, it's the most guarded treasure in my home, the ruler of kitchen tools and a must-have! If you don't love or have a sheet pan, you should. Why? Became it's super easy to use, super easy to clean and your food is ready before you walk into the sitting room and back.

You might be thinking "One-pot meals already do this." True, but one-pot meals have restrictions, unless you don't mind having soup all day every day. It's okay to want and appreciate the simplicity of the famous one-pot meal, but don't you ever think about having more? About getting creative and going crazy with ingredients and still ending up with a tasty and absolutely satisfying meal.

This is where my sheet pan walks in dramatically. It's also called a **rimmed baking sheet** or **a half sheet.** Honestly, I think this versatile kitchen tool deserves more accolades for being able to get together easy and tasty foods at a go! I'm not messing with you. You want some beef stew but can't really be bothered to go through the super long process, so you'd rather get something else. Now you don't have to anymore. Throw some beef into a sheet pan with some buttered carrots and herbed breadcrumbs and just like that, dinner is served!

Sheet pan cooking is the large cooking method umbrella for broiling, roasting and baking because by using these three methods you can concentrate the flavor and even intensify it. I didn't come up with that, science did. I'll explain. A typical sheet pan has shallow sides which were constructed to let the even heat of the oven spread around whatever is inside, let's say chicken breasts. This works to draw out it's natural flavour, which in turn produces a brown but crispy exterior and a surprisingly juicy and soft interior. Like magic, am I right?

All this by throwing a few things onto a pan, sliding it into the oven and shutting it. It even saves you the trouble of constantly stirring the food because we can't have hot oil flying around and possibly staining that pretty shirt you got for a lot of dollars, can we? Plus I personally am not a fan of cleaning oil off of tabletops, so there's that. You also get to finally watch a movie and prepare a delicious meal at the same time. Most meals don't give a lot of room for free time. They're oh so clingy... But not Mr. Sheet Pan here!

What's So Special About The Sheet Pan?

Good question. I asked this once upon a time myself and I didn't exactly have the answers presented to me on a golden platter, so I had to do a little digging on my own. Let's start with the most basic question; what is a sheet pan? A sheet pan or rimmed baking sheet as you already know if you were paying attention is a flat square or rectangular metal pan surrounded by lips roughly 1-inch in size. It is most used to bake things. Cakes, dinner rolls, cookies, meat pies, you name it.

Aluminum and stainless steel are the two things that come to mind when thinking about **making** a sheet pan. A sheet pan for the pros, that is, professional kitchens like the ones restaurants have can be really enormous, say, 26 x 18 inches. In a regular home, it's usually an 18 x 13 inch size that you'll find. It's called a **half sheet** and it gets the job done just the same, but in smaller quantities.

Just a side note: The pans for making jelly rolls are just the same as sheet pans, but a tad smaller and thinner. This means that they can't stand high heat and might warp. Please use a half sheet for the recipes I will list in a minute.

You might even own a sheet pan without ever knowing it. A wedding gift maybe? Rack your brain and kitchen to check. If you don't find one, that's totally fine. Sheet pans can be easily purchased. Any store with kitchen supplies should have it and if they don't, that's a bit shady, it's just a pan!

The point is, you can easily get a sheet pan. If your budget is quite small, check for options online. Honestly, I think you should own two sheey pans. Maybe five, I'm obsessed! You will be at the end of this book.

Tips with a cherry on top

As easy as it is to get a sheet pan, it's not exactly ABC. There are some things to know before picking out a pan that best suits your kitchen. You could try the non-stick pan, although I prefer the regular ones made from stainless steel or aluminium because non-stick pans eventually chip off due to wear and tear. This can be bad business for your food because you don't really know how that will react with the ingredients in your food. Oh well, don't mind me. I'm only assuming you wouldn't like your chicken tenders with a side of nonstick chips, but who knows!

The main reason people get non-stick pans is to avoid the whole shindig of the food sticking to the pan. It happens mostly with sugary fruits, baked stuff and lean beef. A quick remedy is to line your sheet pan with parchment paper or aluminium foil. They are very cheap and easy to use. Plus it saves you more trouble than you realise. Cleaning would be almost too easy, that's one! Get both at any store.

You can also try some olive oil. I use it when dealing with the veggies and roasted meats because they can get pretty clingy sometimes. I drizzle a bit of the oil onto my already lined pan and voila! Problem solved.

If you're feeling a bit fancy, you can throw your money on a non-stick silicone baking mat called silpat. It's quite popular amongst pro bakers and will most definitely look super cool in your kitchen when you're not cleaning it. Yes, you have to clean it after each use, it's not disposable like foil or parchment paper. You also can't cut on them so that rules them out for dishes like pizza, no? I can do without them and by them, I don't mean pizza.

More Reasons To Get A Sheet Pan?

I'm sure you're now well aware of what the sheet pan is and all that. This is the part where you wonder what's in it for you. Apart from all the sciencey stuff and baking logic that says you are sure to get maximum tenderness, juiciness and a lot of flavor plus browning with a pan which are all good things, I must add. I think it's the hands off, super easy and clean method that really does it. I'll give a quick example.

One time I had a date with a pretty boy, say Sam. I loved to cook (still love to) at the time so I figured "hey why not make Sam a fancy dinner." I wanted to impress him; you know what that's like. Another thing I wanted to do was not sweat off my makeup in the process. So I whipped out my humble pan and decided to prepare roast chicken and potatoes with mustard, a total classic. All I had to do was nicely arrange everything on the pan and pop it in the oven. I had to peek into the oven just once, only once.

And the pan said, "let there be roasted chicken and behold, it came to be."

The result was beautifully browned potatoes with a creamy center and crisp, but moist chicken. I was impressed with myself.

And the pan, of course. You best believe I bagged a second date with all that tastiness.

This doesn't mean that the sheet pan got me a date, it means that the job I had to do was relatively easier and I got 70% off the time it would have normally taken to prepare it the usual way. It also helped me enjoy my date. It can do the same for you. Maybe not a date, maybe a weekend with the kids or your grandma. It does it by letting your oven do most of the work while giving you a lot of time for other things. Great food and free time, tell me a better combo. I'll wait.

This book is basically all about preparing easy meals bursting with flavor in the most enjoyable way I know. It can involve a few shortcuts like packaged polenta. I know you might like to make your meals from scratch, I do too but honey, some days are just awful and you won't find the energy or time to start a full meal from the bottom.

Imagine coming home after a long day at work and all you care about is a nice warm bath, any food, really and a lot of sleep. It's easier to junk it up because well, it's quicker but with your sheet pan, you can get a full meal in record time even if it means using a few frozen or jarred ingredients. Unless you want to stand by while a pot of polenta cooks for about an hour...

I guessed so. Anyway, you're in safe hands here because this is a recipe book as you must already know ha-ha! I have recipes for almost every occasion right out of your oven. On board yet? Leggo!

Mistakes You're Likely To Make.

1. **Your sheet pan shouldn't warp on high heat.** It's totally okay to use your mother's pan or any old pan if you like, but if your pan clearly can't stand the heat, it's probably a sign you need a new pan. Some cheap pans have this annoying habit and this can lead to your food ending up on the oven floor. Nobody wants that. Thin baking sheets are not very suitable for the oven, so spare a few bucks and get yourself a proper, thick aluminium half sheet. There are lots of brands to choose from.

2. **We don't steam food here.** Packing a lot of ingredients on the pan does not give enough room for it to breathe and you'll end up with steamed food as opposed to the initial plan, which was browned food. The point is to sear, not steam. Steaming will sort of dilute the flavor and make everything taste like meh. When sheet cooking, leave a lot

of space between the ingredients even if it means using two or more sheet pans for a lot of people. If it's just you, 15 minutes and one pan should do the trick.

3. **That sticky problem.** It's completely normal when your food sticks to the pan, it doesn't mean you did anything wrong. However, there are ways to avoid this very frustrating occurrence. If your pan doesn't have a non-stick coat, you should invest in some aluminium foil or parchment paper. You get to save yourself and your food. I mean, the food will likely turn out okay, but the mess you'll have to clean afterwards won't be worth it unless your favorite hobby is scrubbing the insides of a pan. Get some lining, okay?

4. **Uneven cooking.** Ever tried sheet cooking potatoes and ended up with partly uncooked potatoes? Different ingredients have different cooking rates. You can't expect potatoes and pasta to get cooked at the same time under the same conditions. If you happen to require ingredients with longer cooking times, dice the time up. Chop chop chop. Tiny pieces cook faster. Take pork and asparagus for example, you'll have cut the potatoes into bits and leave the asparagus as whole as a peach. Or you could just cook them in stages starting with the ingredients that take longer and adding the other ones much later, maybe towards the end of the cooking.

5. **Can't find all the flavour you were promised?** Meals prepared through sheet pan cooking are guaranteed to give you a flavour rush, but maybe you don't get it and you automatically conclude that the sheet pan didn't live up to its expectations. Good thing is, this problem can easily be remedied by using more seasoning or marinades. When preparing a sheet pan meal, you need to carefully select ingredients that go together, sorta like shopping. Sheet pan ingredients should naturally taste good when you roast them. There are certain things you just can't roast, a ribeye for example. That should be put on the grill. Do your research, mix the right ingredients and send me a 'thank you' card later.

6. **Burnt and uncooked at different sides.** Ovens are different and tricky. Some ovens work great on the bottom right, but not so good at the top left. If you want to be a sheet pan pro, you'll need to know your oven's hot spots. How? Get an oven thermometer from your local store or online. Make your oven isn't wonky and if it is, get familiar with the wonkiness or just fix it. Another important tip is to swap the pans halfway through cooking, assuming you're using more than one pan. This makes sure the heat spreads evenly and that's a good thing, no?

Have fun with your sheet pan. Don't be scared it'll turn out bad. You'll make mistakes, I know I did. I have a lot of recipes for you to play with. Ready for the recipes yet? Let's get right to it now.

Chapter One: Sheet Pan Pastry Recipes

Oh sweet pastries. What will we do without our floury little friends? It shouldn't be surprising that this is Chapter one. I mean, the whole point behind sheet pan cooking is **baking** and what do we usually associate baking with? Ding ding ding! Pastries. Enough said, let's take a quick look at my all-time favourites.

Cream Puffs

- Prep time: 15 minutes
- Cooking time: 30 minutes
- Serving: 12
- Calories: 116.9 kcal per serving
- Fat: 8.7g|Protein: 2.2g|Carbs: 7.7g|Fiber: 0.1g

INGREDIENTS:

Pastry Cream:

1. Cornstarch (¼ cup)
2. Sugar (¾ cups)
3. Vanilla bean (½ stalk)
4. Whole milk (3 cups)
5. Unsalted butter (4 tablespoons)
6. Egg yolks (4 eggs)
7. Fine sea salt or Kosher salt (¼ teaspoon)
8. Unbleached all-purpose flour (1 tablespoon)

Cream Puff Shells:

1. Fine sea salt or Kosher salt (¼ teaspoon)
2. Water (1 cup)
3. Unbleached all-purpose flour (1 cup)
4. Unsalted butter (½ cup)
5. Whole eggs (4 medium sizes)

Sweetened Whipped Cream:

1. Ground sugar (2 tablespoons)
2. Heavy whipping cream (¾ cup)

INSTRUCTIONS:

1. We're going to start with the pastry cream. Mix a quarter cup of milk, flour, egg yolks and cornstarch in a bowl. When that is all mixed up, set it aside.
2. Whip out a pan. No, not a sheet pan, it's too soon. A saucepan now. Pour in the leftover milk, salt and sugar. Open up the vanilla bean and scrape out the insides with a knife or spoon. Throw both seeds and pod into the pan and set it over medium heat until it boils. Now take it off.
3. Now stir in half of the hot milk mixture into the pastry cream mixture nice and easy. Transfer the new egg-pastry cream mix into the pan and let it heat over medium heat while you steadily stir it until it starts to boil. Stop stirring and let it boil for about 30 seconds before you take if off the heat.
4. Strain mixture through a fund sieve that is set over a bowl. Once you've gotten all the cream through the sieve, it's safe to add butter. Don't stir until the butter is completely melted.
5. Place a large enough piece of plastic wrap right on top of the cream and put it in the fridge for a few hours, depends on your fridge. Make sure to stir before you use it.
6. Now for the **cream puff shells**, prep your oven by preheating to 425°F.
7. Line a sheet pan with parchment paper and set aside.

8. Mix water, salt and butter in a saucepan set over medium high heat until it starts to boil. Take it off heat and stir in all the flour until it's all mixed up. You'll need a lot of strength for this part. And oh, use a wooden spoon.

9. I'm sure you've mixed all the flour nicely. Place the pan right over medium-high heat and stir steadily for 3 minutes or until you get a smooth and shiny dough that also happens to be pulling away from the pan.

10. Run an electric mixer through the dough and set it aside to cool for 5 minutes. Whisk in eggs one by one. When whisking, don't leave out the sides of the bowl. Do this until the eggs are thoroughly mixed. Right after adding the third egg, the mixture should look beaten and a bit fluffy. To check, dip a silicone spatula in the bowl and lift it out with a bit of batter on it. If it doesn't look fluffy enough, add the fourth egg and whisk until it is.

11. Move the batter to a pastry bag. Attach a half inch round tip and go ahead to pipe the batter into about 12 rounds or so on the prepared sheet pan. Wet a finger and press down any peaks you see.

12. Slide it into the oven to bake for about 15 minutes before reducing the heat to 350°F and baking for an extra 15 minutes. If it's done right, the batter should look puffed and risen.

13. Now turn off your oven and open the door a teensy bit. Leave the puffs in the oven for another 20 minutes.

14. Take the puffs out of the oven and slowly but steadily lift them off the sheet and arrange on a wire rack to cool. Use a knife to pierce one side of all the puffs to release steam. Don't fill just yet, it should cool completely.

15. To make sweetened **whipped cream**, put the heavy cream in a bowl and whisk until you see soft peaks form. Pour in sugar and whisk again till the peaks are stiff.

16. For the finishing touch, remove the pastry cream from the refrigerator and stir in the whipped cream until it's completely mixed. Now put the cream inside a piping bag then fit with a large star tip or any shape you want. Just make sure it's a large size.

17. Slice the puff in half and spread the cream all over the bottom half. Put the top half back on and sprinkle with granulated sugar.

18. Serve immediately or store in the fridge. Sprinkle a bit more sugar right before serving.

19. Bon appétit!

Sheet Pan Cornbread

- Prep time: 10 minutes
- Cooking time: 27 minutes
- Serving: 16
- Calories: 138 kcal per serving
- Fat: 4.8g|Protein: 3.1g|Carbs: 21.3g|Fiber: 1g

INGREDIENTS:

1. Baking powder (1 tablespoon)
2. Cooking spray
3. Salt (1¼ teaspoons)

4. All-purpose flour (2½ cups)
5. Lightly beaten whole eggs (4 large sizes)
6. Ground yellow cornmeal (2 cups)
7. Cool melted unsalted butter (6 tablespoons)
8. Buttermilk (2½ cups)

INSTRUCTIONS:

1. Set up a rack in the middle of your oven and preheat to 375°F °
2. Generously spray the sheet pan with some cooking spray and keep it aside.
3. In a large bowl, pour in cornmeal, flour, salt and baking powder. Mix thoroughly.
4. Use your fingers to make a nice well in the middle of your dry mixture and pour in butter, buttermilk and eggs. Now go ahead to stir until it's properly mixed.
5. Transfer this mixture onto your coated sheet pan and spread it out with a spatula to get a nice even layer.
6. Slide pan in the oven to bake for about 27 minutes. It should have a nice golden brown tone and should be pulling away from the edges of the pan.
7. When it's ready, leave to cool for a bit before you slice into 16 pieces and serve with some extra butter if you like.

Garlic Bread With Grilled Cheese

- Prep time: 20 minutes
- Cooking time: 10 minutes
- Serving: 4
- Calories: 258 kcal per serving
- Fat: 14.1g|Protein: 8.7g|Carbs: 23.3g|Fiber: 0g

INGREDIENTS:

1. Shredded cheddar cheese (⅓ cup)
2. Land O Lakes butter plus canola oil (½ cup)
3. Bakery sandwich bread (8 slices)
4. Shredded parmesan cheese (⅓ cup)
5. Garlic and herb cheese spread (¼ cup)
6. Land O Lakes deli American (8 slices)

INSTRUCTIONS:

1. Prepare oven by preheating to 450°F.
2. In a small bowl, pour in shredded parmesan cheese and butter. Mix thoroughly and set aside.
3. Get a slice of bread and evenly spread some butter mixture on one side of it. About a tablespoon. Do this to four slices.
4. Put the buttered slices on the sheet pan with the buttered side facing down. Place two slices of Deli American and a quarter cup of shredded cheddar cheese on each slice.
5. To the remaining slices without butter, spread a tablespoon of garlic and herb cheese spread and place it on top of the other buttered slices with the cheese spread side facing down.
6. Slide in the oven to bake for 5 minutes before flipping and baking for another 5 or 6 minutes. The cheese should be melted and the bread, brown.
7. Serve warm.

Easy Sourdough Bread

- Prep time: 12 hours 10 minutes
- Cooking time: 45 minutes
- Serving: 30 slices
- Calories: 127kcal per serving
- Fat: 1.2g|Protein: 4g|Carbs: 26g|Fiber: 2.5g

INGREDIENTS:

1. All-purpose flour (4¼ cups)
2. Sourdough starter (⅔ cup)
3. Salt (2 teaspoons)
4. Lukewarm water (1⅓ cups)

INSTRUCTIONS:

1. Pour all ingredients into a bowl and stir thoroughly until you get a loosely mixed and chunky dough.
2. Drop the dough on a flat surface and work through the dough with your hands, kneading until its smooth). How to knead? Just stretch and massage the dough to help work on the gluten. Now it should feel sticky and wet. Whatever you do, do not add extra flour or you'll end up with heavy hard bread. It's okay if the doughy sticks to your hands and make you feel messy. Just wet your hands a bit so it won't stick so much.
3. Transfer the dough to a boil with the insides coated in oil. Place plastic wrap over it and let the dough sit in the fridge overnight or for 4-6 hours at room temperature. If you don't have a plastic wrap, use a towel. It will have a more sourdough kinda tangy flavor of you leave it for longer in the refrigerator.
4. Transfer the dough from the bowl back onto the flat surface and punch the air out of it.
5. Use your hands to form a ball out of it.
6. Put the dough balls in any container you'd like to shape it into and leave it to rise again in the refrigerator overnight or for another 4-6 hours at room temperature.
7. Heat your oven to 450°F.
8. Place the loaf of bread on a sheet pan, slash it with a knife and slide it into the oven to bake for 45 minutes.

Sheet Pan French Toast Bake

- Prep time: 15 minutes
- Cooking time: 30 minutes
- Serving: 9
- Calories: 258kcal per serving
- Fat: 11.1g|Protein: 6.6g|Carbs: 39g|Fiber: 2.3g

INGREDIENTS:

1. Milk (2 cups)
2. Dark brown sugar (½ cup)
3. Vanilla extract (1 teaspoon)
4. Unsalted butter (1 cup)
5. Halved toasted pecans (1 cup)
6. Nutmeg powder (¼ teaspoon)
7. Granulated sugar
8. Whisked eggs (5 whole eggs)
9. Cinnamon powder (1 teaspoon)
10. Loaf of Italian bread (9 huge slices)
11. Warm maple syrup

INSTRUCTIONS:

1. Prepare oven by preheating to 350°F.
2. Pour butter, halved pecans and dark brown sugar onto a large sheet pan the slide pan in the oven to melt the butter. This should take 5 minutes.
3. Take out the pan and whisk the dark sugar, pecans and melted butter, doing well to spread it across the sheet pan to create an even layer. Set aside
4. Get a large bowl and pour in vanilla extract, nutmeg powder, whisked eggs, milk and cinnamon powder. Mix thoroughly.
5. Dip the bread slices in the milk mixture and arrange then on the dark sugar mixture in the sheet pan.
6. Put the pan in the oven, center rack and back for 15 minutes uncovered. Flip the slices and bake for an extra 15 minutes. The edges should look crisp.
7. Serve warm with a light drizzle of maple syrup. Sprinkle granulated sugar over that and enjoy!

Classic Focaccia Bread

- Prep time: 12 hours
- Cooking time: 35 minutes
- Serving: 1 loaf
- Calories: 171 kcal
- Fat: 9.9g|Protein: 9g|Carbs: 64.4g|Fiber: 2.6g

INGREDIENTS:

1. Active dry yeast (2¼ teaspoons)
2. Extra virgin olive oil (5 teaspoon + extra for glazing)
3. Sugar (¼ teaspoon)
4. Bread flour (6¼ cups)
5. Morton kosher salt (1 tablespoon) or Diamond crystal salt (2 tablespoons)
6. Flaky sea salt

INSTRUCTIONS:

1. Mix bread flour and 2 ½ cups of water in a stand mixer bowl. The water must be room temperature. Fit the dough hook and spin on low speed, doing well to scrape the sides so that all the dry flour get mixed up to form a shaggy dough.
2. Take off the dough hook and place plastic wrap over the bowl. Leave it to sit while you prepare the yeast. It can stay for at most, 2 hours.
3. To prepare yeast, pour sugar, half a cup of warm water and yeast into a bowl. Stir with a fork until it dissolves. Set aside to sit for 5 minutes or until it looks frothy.
4. Transfer prepared yeast into the bowl of the stand mixer and spin on low until all the excess water has been absorbed by the dough. Takes a minute. To avoid splashing water everywhere and on yourself, pulse and stop a few times in the beginning.
5. Sprinkle Kosher salt and spin again. Raise the speed to medium and let it spin for 5 minutes. This will make the dough very elastic and sticky. It should stick to the sides of the bowl like a typical thick batter if done right.
6. Drizzle exactly 3 tablespoons of oil into a large glass bowl and swirl the bowl around so the oil gets everywhere.
7. Place the dough inside this bowl. Make sure to get as much dough inside as you can. Use a spatula, does the job.
8. Place plastic wrap over it and leave it to rise in a warm place for 2 or 3 hours. The dough should have doubled in size by them. To monitor the increase, mark the exact position of the dough on the glass bowl before you leave it to rise. A knife would ruin your bowl, so use paper tape.
9. Coat your sheet in oil using your fingers. Be sure to get oil on the sides too.
10. Remove the plastic wrap covering the dough and fold it a few times to release air. By it, I mean the dough and not the wrap.
11. Move it to the coated sheet pan and fold it onto itself like in meat pie. Oil your hands first so it doesn't get sticky and messy.
12. Turn the sheet to the other side and fold again.
13. Coat a plastic wrap in oil and cover the dough. Again. Just 10 minutes this time, I promise.
14. Remove the wrap and carefully stretch the dough with your oiled hands to cover the entire surface of the sheet pan. Be gentle so you don't tear it and if it doesn't stay stretched, leave it alone for about 10 minutes and try again.
15. Put another oiled plastic wrap over it and leave it to chill overnight or 8 hours.
16. Now move the sheet pan to a warm place for 1 hour 5 minutes. This will double the dough and make it puffed. In a standard half sheet, the dough should to the top.
17. Now prepare your oven at 450°F.
18. Move the oven rack to the center.
19. Take off the plastic wrap and coat the dough with enough oil. Coat your hands too because you'll be using them to press the dough all the way down.

20. Sprinkle the top with enu sea salt and slide it in the oven to bake for 35 minu[...] should have a deep brown tinge.
21. When it's ready, leave it in the pan to cool for 10 minutes before removing it with [...] help of a thin metal spatula.
22. Let it cool on a wire rack before slicing and serving

heet Pan Cuban Sandwiches

- Prep time: 10 minutes
- Cooking time: 20 minutes
- Serving: 8
- Calories: 670 kcal
- Fat: 24.6g|Protein: 23.8g|Carbs: 49.4g|Fiber: 5.9g

INGREDIENTS:

1. Yellow mustard (½ cup)
2. Soft French bread (2 loaves sliced in half)
3. Fully cooked smoked ham, sliced (2/4 lb.)
4. Olive oil (1 tablespoon)
5. Swiss cheese (24 slices)
6. Pickle juice (4 teaspoons)
7. Fully cooked pork roast, sliced (1½ lb.)
8. Dill pickle chips (2½ cups)

INSTRUCTIONS:

1. Prep oven by preheating to 400°F.
2. Coat the sheet pan with a teaspoon and a half of oil.
3. Put the bread bottoms on top of the coated sheet and spread some yellow mustard on them. About a tablespoon each.
4. You're now going to place three swiss cheese slices right on top of that. Then the pork, pickles and ham right on top of that. Three more slices of Swiss cheese on top of that.
5. Now on the top bread slices, spread a teaspoon of pickle juice each and the leftover yellow mustard. Cover the bottom slice with the top slice and glaze with the remaining oil.
6. Get another sheet pan and place it on top of the sandwich. Put two cast iron skillets on them to press the sandwiches a little bit.
7. Now gently place that setup, skillet and all, inside the oven and leave to bake for 20 minutes. The bread should be brown and the cheese, melted.
8. Slice the sandwiches into 8 pieces and serve warm.

Herbed Oatmeal Pan Bread

- Prep time: 2 hours
- Cooking time: 25 minutes
- Serving: 30
- Calories: 212 kcal
- Fat: 12g|Protein: 11g|Carbs: 68g|Fiber: 4g

INGREDIENTS:

1. Old fashioned oats (1 cup)
2. Sugar (¼ cup)
3. Hot water (1 cup)
4. Lightly beaten whole egg (1 large
5. Active dry yeast (2 packages)
6. Softened butter (3 tablespoons)
7. All-purpose flour (4 cups)
8. Salt (2 teaspoons)

9. Warm water (½ cup)

Topping:

1. Dried basil leaves (1 teaspoon)
2. Melted butter (¼ cup)
3. Dried oregano (½ teaspoon)
4. Grated parmesan cheese (2 tablespoons)
5. Garlic powder (½ teaspoon)

INSTRUCTIONS:

1. Pour hot water in a small bowl, stir in old fashioned oats and set aside.
2. In a bigger bowl, mix yeast and warm water until yeast dissolves. Pour in salt, sugar, butter, oat mixture, 2 cups of flour and eggs. Whisk until it looks smooth.
3. Pour in enough flour and mix again until it forms a soft dough.
4. Sprinkle some flour on a hard flat surface. Transfer the dough to said surface and knead for about 8 minutes. Your dough should be smooth and elastic.
5. Move the dough to an oiled bowl. Flip it to grease the other side.
6. Place plastic wrap over it and leave it to rise in a warm spot for 45 minutes. If it hasn't doubled in size, leave it for longer.
7. Transfer dough to the sheet pan and press it all the way to the bottom so it spreads out and forms an even layer.
8. Slice through the dough horizontally using a sharp knife. Do the same vertically leaving you with a square shaped pattern.
9. Place plastic wrap over it again and let it rise for just an hour.
10. Use the knife to redefine the square pattern before glazing tops with some melted butter.
11. Slide it in the oven to bake for 15 minutes at 375°F.
12. While that is happening, mix basil, garlic powder, parmesan cheese and oregano in a bowl.
13. Glaze the top of the bread with a little more butter, sprinkle the cheese mixture over it and bake again for about 5 minutes.
14. Place aluminum foil over the pan and bake for an additional 5 minutes.
15. Serve!

Classic White Bread

- Prep time:8 hours
- Cooking time: 40 minutes
- Serving: 1 loaf
- Calories: 210kcal
- Fat: 3.5g|Protein: 6g|Carbs: 36g|Fiber: 1g

INGREDIENTS:

1. Lukewarm water (1 cup)
2. Olive oil (2 tablespoons)
3. White granulated sugar (1 tablespoon)
4. Salt (1 teaspoon)
5. Yeast (2 ½ teaspoons)
6. All-purpose flour (2 ½ cups)

INSTRUCTIONS:

1. You're going to prepare the yeast first. Pour yeast and granulated sugar into the cup of lukewarm water and stir to dissolve. If you're adding anything extra, you'll need to leave it to sit for about 6-12 minutes or until the yeast clearly comes alive. If it's just yeast, no need for all that. You can just carry on or still let it for a while so you'd be sure the yeast is alive and well.
2. Pour flour into a medium sized bowl and stir in salt.
3. Pour wet ingredients (yeast mixture) into dry ingredients (flour mixture) and mix thoroughly until a dough forms.
4. Powder a hard flat surface with some flour and drop the dough onto it. Knead gently for 2 minutes, sprinkle some flour when needed to make sure it does not stick.
5. Don't over knead, just do it enough for it to be a cohesive mixture. It doesn't have to be elastic or lumpy. Now powder your hands and scoop a bit of the dough to form a ball.
6. Coat a Ziplock bag with some olive oil and drop the dough ball in it and swirl to coat. Lock it and refrigerate for 8 hours or overnight, preferably.
7. When the time is up, remove the bag from the fridge and massage the dough ball through the bag to release all the air trapped inside. Unzip the bag to let the air out but be sure to zip it up right after.
8. Place the bag anywhere you like in your kitchen as long as it is room temperature. Leave the dough to sit for 1 hour to rise and double in volume.
9. Prepare your oven by preheating to 350°F.
10. Powder the bottom of a sheet pan with some corn flour and set aside
11. Powder the surface of a flat hard surface again and place the dough on it. Squeeze out as much olive oil as you can from the Ziplock bag. Not necessarily everything, just enough.
12. Knead the dough and try to fold in the olive oil as much as you can.
13. Transfer the dough to your sheet pan and press it in if it doesn't fit.
14. Put a plastic wrap over the pan and leave it to rise until it is obviously double its original size even if it goes past the top of the pan
15. Take out the plastic wrap, slide sheet pan in the oven and leave to bake for 40 minutes at 350°F. The result should be golden brown and should produce a hollow sound when you tap it.
16. Transfer the loaf to a wire rack to cool before slicing and serving.
17. Enjoy!

Chapter Two: Sheet Pan Breakfast Recipes

For a long time, sheet pan meals have been restricted to only dinner time and while that's great because sheet pan meals are just great, there's a lot more than can be done with the pan. Chicken and veggies taste awesome, but where is your sense of adventure? The power of the pan is slowly seeping into the early morning rush and I am all for it. Welcome to the new age.

Sheet Pan Hash Browns and Eggs

- Prep time: 5 minutes
- Cooking time: 50 minutes
- Serving: 6
- Calories: 180 kcal
- Fat: 12g|Protein: 11g|Carbs: 12g|Fiber: 1g

INGREDIENTS:

1. Chopped onions (¾ cup)
2. Vegetable oil cooking spray
3. Garlic powder (1 teaspoon)
4. Whole eggs (6 large sizes)
5. Frozen shredded hash browns (1 bag)
6. Real bacon bits (¼ cup)
7. Salt (¼ teaspoon)
8. Chopped green pepper (¾ cup)
9. Black pepper powder (¼ teaspoon)
10. Onion powder (1 teaspoon)
11. Snipped chives (3 tablespoons)

INSTRUCTIONS:

1. Prepare your oven by preheating to 400°F.
2. Coat the inside of your sheet pan with cooking spray and arrange frozen hash browns, green pepper and chopped onions on the coated sheet. Coat all sides with cooking spray by spraying and tossing
3. Sprinkle onion powder and garlic powder. Toss to mix.
4. Slide the sheet pan in the oven and leave to bake for about 45-50 minutes depending on how crispy you want them to be.
5. Bring them out of the oven and pour in bacon bits. Stir.
6. Make 6 hash brown nests and crack open an egg straight into each nest. Each nest should have a whole cracked egg.
7. Put the pan back in the oven and bake for about 6 minutes or less if you want a sunny-side up kind of egg. If you want a thoroughly cooked egg, leave it for an extra 2 minutes in the oven.
8. Take it out of the oven and season with pepper and salt. Serve with chive garnish.

Crustless Spinach Quiche

- Prep time: 20 minutes
- Cooking time: 30 minutes
- Serving: 6
- Calories: 309 kcal
- Fat: 11.2g|Protein: 18g|Carbs: 6.1g |Fiber: 1.5g

INGREDIENTS:

1. Chopped onion (1 large size)
2. Beaten eggs (5 whole eggs)
3. Salt (¼ teaspoon)
4. Vegetable oil (1 tablespoon)
5. Frozen chopped spinach (1 package). It should be thawed and drained before use.
6. Black pepper powder (⅛ teaspoon)
7. Shredded Muenster cheese (3 cups)

INSTRUCTIONS:

1. Prepare your oven by preheating to 350°F.
2. Coat your sheet pan with cooking spray or some vegetable oil.
3. Drizzle the oil in a large pan and place it over medium it. Stir in onions and let cook until it is soft.
4. Add spinach and leave to cook until it's a bit dried up. This is because all the unnecessary moisture has gone up and away.
5. Beat eggs in a large bowl. Add pepper, salt and shredded cheese. Stir in spinach mixture until it's completely mixed.
6. Pour mixture onto greased pan and slide it into the oven.
7. Leave it to bake for 30 minutes or extra for the eggs to set.
8. Set it aside to cool for about 5 minutes or more.
9. Serve warm.

Disco Fries

- Prep time: 25 minutes
- Cooking time: 10 minutes
- Serving: 4
- Calories: 334kcal
- Fat: 15.5g|Protein: 18.9g|Carbs: 24.6g|Fiber: 2.5g

INGREDIENTS:

1. Bacon strips (4 thick slices)
2. Beef broth (½ cup)
3. Brewed coffee (½ cup)
4. Black pepper powder (¼ teaspoon)
5. Frozen French fries (1 package)
6. Diced white onions (½ cup)
7. Tomato juice (¼ cup)
8. All-purpose flour (1 tablespoon)
9. Fried eggs (3 whole eggs)
10. Whole milk (½ cup)
11. Kosher salt (¼ teaspoon)
12. Bite-size American cheese (5 slices)
13. Minced fresh chives (2 tablespoons)

INSTRUCTIONS:

1. First thing to do is bake French fries according to manufacturer's directions.
2. While that is happening, pour bacon into a nonstick pan and place it over medium heat to cook. Stir it every now and then for 10 minutes or until it's crispy enough.
3. Move cooked bacon to a place lined with some paper towels. Leave whatever oil is left in the pan where it is, you'll need it for this next step.
4. Throw onions into pan and stir for 2 minutes or until it looks translucent. Pour in flour and stir for 2 minutes until you get a nice flour-onion mixture.
5. Now pour in coffee, milk, tomato juice and broth. Stir every once in a while until the mixture thickens. This usually takes 15 minutes.
6. Season with salt and pepper and then turn off the heat. Leave the lid on so it stays warm.
7. Pour shredded cheese on top of the French fries and slide it back in the oven to bake until cheese melts. It should bake for 2 minutes at 425°F.
8. Top with bacon, gravy and fried eggs.
9. Serve with chives sprinkled all over it.

Slab Quiche

- Prep time: 30 minutes
- Cooking time: 40 minutes
- Serving: 6
- Calories: 334kcal
- Fat: 24.6|Protein: 9.9g|Carbs: 19.7g|Fiber: 1.7g

INGREDIENTS:

1. Extra virgin olive oil (3 tablespoons)
2. Thawed frozen puff pastry (1 sheet)
3. Sliced red onion (1 medium size)
4. Egg yolks (2 large sizes)
5. Chopped fresh thyme leaves (1 teaspoon)
6. Crumbles fresh goat cheese (½ cup)
7. All-purpose flour
8. Whole eggs (2 large sizes)
9. Freshly shredded gruyere cheese
10. Kosher salt (1 teaspoon)
11. Heavy whipping cream (½ cup)
12. Roughly cut fresh spinach (2 cups)
13. Whole milk (1 cup)
14. Ground pepper powder (½ teaspoon)

INSTRUCTIONS:

1. First thing you're going to do is move the oven rack to the bottom middle level and turn on the heat to 300°F.
2. Put the chopped red onion in a rimmed sheet pan and drizzle olive oil all over it. Sprinkle thyme and toss to coat.
3. Now spread it all out in a nice even layer and place aluminium foil over it making sure to seal the edges.
4. Place said pan in the oven and roast for 20 minutes or until they're obviously soft.
5. Remove the foil and begin to stir, still cooking the onions until they look brown and soft, even sticky. 20 minutes tops.
6. Take the pan out of the oven and season onions with salt. Move them to a plate to properly cool.
7. Set the oven to 400°F.
8. Powder a hard flat surface and place the pastry on it. Gently roll out the pastry to a quarter inch thick and place it on the sheet pan. Prick the dough with a fork and put the sheet pan in the fridge to set while you start on the filling.
9. In a fairly large bowl, mix whole eggs and egg yolks. Stir in cream, pepper, milk and the remaining teaspoon of salt.
10. Take the dough out of the fridge and pour half of the gruyere on it and spread it around using a spatula.
11. Sprinkle onions, then spinach and the remaining gruyere.
12. Layer with egg filling and crumbled goat cheese.
13. Slide pan into the oven to bake for about 10 minutes.
14. Lower the heat and bake for an extra 25 minutes. The fill should be set around the edges now.
15. Turn on the broiler and move the oven rack to the highest position along with the sheet pan. Broil for a minute or until quiche is evenly browned.
16. Slice and serve warm.

Perfect Bacon in the Oven

- Prep time: 5 minutes
- Cooking time: 29 minutes
- Serving: 6
- Calories: 473 kcal
- Fat: 43.27g|Protein: 35g|Carbs: 1.35g|Fiber: 0g

INGREDIENTS:

1. Sliced bacon (2 pounds)

EQUIPMENT:

1. Tongs
2. Aluminium foil
3. Platter
4. Rimmed sheet pan
5. Paper towels

CTIONS:

1. Prepare your oven by preheating to 400°F.
2. Set the oven rack to the lower third position and leave to heat. If you're making more than one sheet of bacon, place a second rack right over that one.
3. Place bacon on sheet pan lined with aluminium foil. Cleanup will be a total breeze.
4. Bacon should be arranged in a single layer, close together but most definitely not overlapping each other because it'll start to stick when the cooking starts.
5. Put the bacon in the oven and bake until it starts to look golden brown and very crispy. The thickness of the bacon will determine just how much time it'll take to cook through but the usual is 20 minutes. Leave it alone for 12 minutes then start checking, making sure your bacon ja cooking and isn't burning. It will cook in its own fat, so don't worry about adding any extra oil.
6. When it's ready, remove the bacon oil and move the bacon to a plate with paper towels to drain the excess that managed to hang on for dear life. Use tongs for this because it must be really hot at this point.
7. Serve warm.

Chocolate Chip Sheet Pan Pancakes

- Prep time: 15 minutes
- Cooking time: 15 minutes
- Serving: 16
- Calories: 146.6 kcal
- Fat: 2g|Protein: 0g|Carb: 5g|Fiber: 0g

INGREDIENTS:

1. All-purpose flour (⅓ cup)
2. Cooking spray
3. Melted butter (2 tablespoons)
4. Semisweet chocolate chips (3 cups)
5. Syrup
6. Pancake batter and extra ingredients required by the manufacturer (4 cups)

INSTRUCTIONS:

1. Prepare oven by preheating to 425°F.
2. Use some aluminium foil to line a sheet pan and then coat the foil with cooking spray.
3. Get a small bowl, preferably a shallow one, mix chocolate chips with flour until it's thoroughly coated. This will help avoid sinking.
4. Prepare the batter just like the manufacturer says so read the instructions very well.
5. Now pour in the chocolate chips and fold it in.
6. Spread batter out on a sheet pan and bake for 15 minutes or until toothpick comes out slightly moist.
7. The top should look golden in about an extra 3 minutes.
8. Glaze the top with melted butter and serve in slices with syrup.

Chapter Three: Sheet Pan Lunch Recipes

Sheet Pan Shrimp Fajitas

- Prep time: 10 minutes
- Cooking time: 13 minutes
- Serving: 4
- Calories: 246kcal
- Fat: 4g|Protein: 43g|Carbs: 7.5g|Fiber: 2g

INGREDIENTS:

Fajitas:

1. Extra virgin olive oil (2 tablespoons)
2. Oregano (1 teaspoon)
3. Peeled raw shrimp with the veins removed (1lb.)
4. Smoked paprika (½ teaspoon)
5. Cayenne pepper (⅛ teaspoon)
6. Julienned bell peppers (2 cups)
7. Ground cumin (1 teaspoon)
8. Onion powder (¼ teaspoon)
9. Sliced white onions (1 cup)
10. Sea salt (½ teaspoon)

Pilo de Gallo:

1. Fresh lime juice (1 tablespoon)
2. Chopped tomatoes (1 cup)
3. Chopped cilantro (¼ cup)
4. Sea salt (¼ teaspoon)
5. Chopped red onion (¼ cup)

Serving:

- Corn tortillas (4)
- Lime wedges (1 medium size)

INSTRUCTIONS:

1. Prepare your oven by preheating to 425°F.
2. Get a sheet pan and line it with some parchment paper. Set it aside.
3. Throw shrimp, onions, dried seasonings, bell peppers and olive oil into a mixing bowl. Stir thoroughly to coat everything in olive oil and seasoning.
4. Pour mixture onto sheet pan and spread out to form an even layer.
5. Slide the pan into the oven and bake for about 8 minutes.
6. Toss and bake for an extra 5 minutes.
7. Serve over tortillas with Pico de Gallo toppings, lime and cilantro

Spring Roll Flavors With Savory Pork And Gluten-free Wrapper

- Prep time: 15 minutes
- Cooking time: 40 minutes
- Serving: 5
- Calories: 103kcal
- Fat: 4g|Protein: 6.3g|Carbs: 10.1g|Fiber: 0.4g

INGREDIENTS:

1. Diced red onion (½ cup)
2. Minced ginger (1 tablespoon)
3. Cooking spray
4. Tamari (1 tablespoon)
5. Minced garlic (2 cloves)
6. Shredded carrots (2 medium sizes)
7. Rice paper (10 wraps)
8. White pepper (¼ teaspoon)
9. Sliced snap peas (¼ pound)
10. Ground pork (½ pound)
11. Water (¼ cup)
12. Minced ginger (1 tablespoon)
13. Extra virgin olive oil (1 tablespoon)

INSTRUCTIONS:

1. Prepare oven as usual by preheating to 375°F.
2. Coat a sheet pan generously with non-stick cooking spray. When that's all done, set it aside.
3. Drizzle oil into a saucepan and stir-fry onions over medium heat for 3 minutes. Stir in garlic and ginger. Leave it to cook for about a minute or until the fragrance fills your kitchen.
4. Throw in white pepper, pork and tamari, stirring to break up pork into pieces. Do this with a wooden spoon for 7 minutes. Set a timer if you must.
5. Stir in snap peas and carrots.
6. Pour water in a shallow pot wide enough for you to put in the rice paper. Now place the rice paper in the pot of water one by one and leave for 20 seconds before transferring to a clean dry surface.
7. Spread out a rice paper and place a tablespoon of pork mixture, a few shredded carrots and sliced snap peas in the center. Fold from top to bottom to cover the filling. Now fold the sides and roll it sort of like a burrito. Repeat with all the rice paper.
8. Place rolls on the sheet pan gently to avoid tearing. Glaze the top evenly with olive oil and slide into the oven to bake.
9. This should cook for 12 minutes before flipping and cooking for another 12 minutes. If done right, it should look a bit golden and translucent.
10. Remove from oven and serve warm.

Healthy Salmon & Veggies

- Prep time: 10 minutes
- Cooking time: 30 minutes
- Serving: 2
- Calories: 500 kcal
- Fat: 14.1g|Protein: 30.9g|Carbs: 26.1g|Fiber: 5.0g

INGREDIENTS:

1. Asparagus (1 pound)
2. Fresh dill (2 teaspoons)
3. Baby potatoes (2 cups)
4. Extra virgin olive oil (1 tablespoon)
5. Salmon (10 oz.)
6. Salt (⅛ teaspoon)
7. Lemon wedges (2)
8. Garlic powder ̶1/8 teaspoon)

INSTRUCTIONS:

1. Prepare the oven by preheating to 450°F .
2. Now proceed to line a sheet pan with parchment paper and set aside.
3. Slice the potatoes in half from the top and throw them in a mixing bowl. Drizzle olive oil over it and toss to mix.
4. Sprinkle garlic powder and salt. Toss again.
5. Pour potatoes onto the sheet pan and spread them out so they bake evenly.
6. Slide the pan into the oven and bake for about 20 minutes.
7. Meanwhile, you have some free time on your hands so why not chop the dill and trim the asparagus.
8. Place the salmon with the skin down on another sheet pan and sprinkle dill, pepper and salt over it.
9. Place asparagus right beside seasoned salmon and bake for roughly 10 minutes.
10. Drizzle lemon juice over the salmon and serve with baked potatoes.

Easy Sesame-glazed Roast Veggies

- Prep time: 10 minutes
- Cooking time: 25 minutes
- Serving: 4
- Calories: 160 kcal
- Fat: 7g|Protein: 4g|Carbs: 19g|Fiber: 6g

INGREDIENTS:

1. Red onion (1 medium size)
2. Garlic powder (½ teaspoon)
3. Red bell pepper (1 medium size)
4. Soy sauce, low sodium (¼ cup)
5. Green bell pepper (1 medium size)
6. Sesame oil (2 tablespoons)
7. Broccoli florets (4 cups)
8. Ground ginger (¼ teaspoon)
9. Raw honey (2 tablespoons)

INSTRUCTIONS:

1. Prepare oven by preheating to 425°F.
2. Get a sheet pan lined with parchment paper and set aside.
3. Dice the pepper and onions. Use your fingers to separate the onion layers.
4. Get a large bowl and mix honey, low sodium soy sauce, sesame oil, garlic powder, honey and ginger powder. Mix thoroughly.
5. Throw in broccoli florets, pepper and onions and mix well.
6. Transfer the vegetables to the lined baking sheet, spreading them out to get an even layer.
7. Slide sheet pan into the oven and bake for roughly 25 minutes.
8. Let the veggies cool for a bit before serving.
9. Enjoy!

Juicy Oven-Baked Cajun Chicken Breasts

- Prep time: 10 minutes
- Cooking time: 20 minutes
- Serving: 4
- Calories: 310 kcal
- Fat: 0.2g|Protein: 3.2g|Carbs: 33.6g|Fiber: 2.3g

INGREDIENTS:

1. Ground garlic (1 teaspoon)
2. Dried thyme powder (1 teaspoon)
3. Onion powder (1 teaspoon)
4. Cayenne pepper (½ teaspoon)
5. Skinned chicken breast (2 pounds)
6. Paprika (2 teaspoons)
7. Dried oregano (1 teaspoon)
8. Extra virgin olive oil (4 tablespoons)
9. Salt (1 teaspoon)
10. Black pepper powder (1 teaspoon)
11. Cooking spray

INSTRUCTIONS:

1. Set your oven to 425°F.
2. Prepare a sheet pan, line it with aluminum foil and coat the foil with cooking spray.
3. Get a mixing bowl. Pour in garlic powder, paprika, black pepper, onion powder, dried oregano, salt, dried thyme and cayenne pepper. Mix thoroughly.
4. Use the spice mixture above to coat the chicken breasts before spreading then out on the lined sheet pan.
5. Drizzle some olive oil on top of the chicken breasts and slide the pan into the oven to bake.
6. Let them bake for about 20 minutes.
7. Take the sheet pan out of the oven and allow it to cool for 5 minutes.
8. Serve warm.

30-Minute Sheet Pan Chicken Caprese

- Prep time: 15 minutes
- Cooking time: 30 minutes
- Serving: 4
- Calories: 310 kcal
- Fat: 2.6g|Protein: 26.3g|Carbs: 10.1g|Fiber: 0.2g

INGREDIENTS:

1. Melted butter (1 tablespoon)
2. Fresh mozzarella cheese (6 oz.)
3. Chicken breasts (24 oz.)
4. Black pepper powder
5. Tomato (1 large size)
6. Salt (1 ½ teaspoon)
7. Basil leaves (4)
8. Italian seasoning (½ teaspoon)
9. Asparagus (1½ pounds)
10. Balsamic vinegar reduction (2 tablespoons)
11. Garlic powder (¼ teaspoon)
12. Sea salt flakes

INSTRUCTIONS:

1. Set oven to 400°F.
2. Prepare a sheet pan, line it with parchment paper.
3. Use as many paper towels as you need to pat the chicken dry before sprinkling with black pepper powder and salt.
4. Pour garlic powder, Italian seasoning and melted butter in a bowl and mix thoroughly.
5. Glaze both sides of the chicken with the butter mixture and spread them out on one side of the sheet pan
6. Use a knife or kitchen scissors to trim the rough asparagus ends and just throw them in a large bowl.
7. Season with half teaspoon of salt, olive oil and black pepper. Mix gently to evenly coat the asparagus with the seasoned oil.
8. Now spread that out on the other side of the sheet pan
9. Put the sheet pan on the middle rack of the oven and leave to bake for 12 minutes.
10. Time to cut the tomato! Use a sharp knife if you're sure you won't cut yourself. Cut the tomato into quarters.
11. Do the same to the mozzarella ball.
12. 12 minutes should be up now, so bring out your sheet pan, put 2 tomatoes slices on each breast. Layer mozzarella rounds over that.
13. Turn the asparagus so the other side can bake as well. It doesn't have to be perfect, just get a rubber spatula and toss.
14. Slide sheet pan back in the oven and bake for an extra 15 minutes. The mozzarella should have melted by now and the chicken should be thoroughly cooked.
15. Take the sheet pan out of the oven and set aside.
16. Arrange the basil leaves in your hand to form a tight log. Now cut through the log in thin slices.
17. Pour balsamic vinegar reduction over the chicken and top with chopped basil.
18. Season with sea salt and serve warm.

Loaded Juicy Lucy Sheet Pan Sliders

- Prep time: 30 minutes
- Cooking time: 40 minutes
- Serving: 12
- Calories: 466kcal
- Fat: 20g|Protein: 34g|Carbs: 31g|Fiber: 0g

INGREDIENTS:

Burgers:

1. Kosher salt (1 tablespoon)
2. Grated onion (½ cup)
3. Lean ground beef (2¼ pounds)
4. American cheese (6 slices)
5. Sharp cheddar cheese (6 slices)
6. Worcestershire sauce (2 teaspoon)
7. Raw bacon (12 strips)
8. Black pepper powder (2 teaspoons)
9. Mozzarella cheese (6 slices)

Burger Sauce:

1. Hot sauce (2 teaspoons)
2. Mayonnaise (¼ cup)
3. Thousand island dressing (¼ cup)

Assembling:

1. Green lettuce (4 large leaves)
2. Dill pickle chips
3. Brioche slider buns (12)
4. Sliced tomatoes (2 medium sizes)

INSTRUCTIONS:

1. Prepare the oven by preheating to 400°F.
2. Line a sheet pan with parchment paper or just spray with nonstick cooking spray.
3. Mix the ground beef, Worcestershire sauce, salt, grated onion and peppers in a large mixing bowl. Mix thoroughly until the ground beef is thoroughly seasoned.
4. Place half of the seasoned beef on the pan and top with the cheeses in rows making sure to leave a bit of room at the edges to avoid any cheesy leakages while the burgers bake. Place the remaining beef mixture on top of the cheese.
5. Here you're going to weave your bacon right on top of your pan. Don't forget to tuck any stray edges. Place your small sheet pan gently on top of a much larger one to catch any grease that might drip during baking.
6. Slide the sheet pan into the oven and cool for roughly 30 minutes or extra if it's not completely cooked through.
7. Turn on your broiler and cook until your bacon is cooked through and crisp.
8. Meanwhile, free time means you get to prepare other things. You'll be making a burger sauce now. In a small bowl, mix the hot sauce, thousand island dressing and mayonnaise. Mix thoroughly and set aside.
9. Place lettuce and tomatoes on the bottom part of the slider buns. Set aside until the burger is done cooking. Drain any excess oil and using a pair of tongs, place the burger right on top of lettuce and tomatoes. If you're going to use pickle chips, this is where they come in.
10. Pour burger sauce all over the burger (and pickle chips) and layer the top part of the slider buns on it.
11. Alice through the rows and columns of the slider buns so that they can be easily separated.
12. Serve warm.

Sheet Pan Garlic Lemon Salmon

- Prep time: 5 minutes
- Cooking time: 20 minutes
- Serving: 4
- Calories: 680kcal
- Fat: 49g|Carbs: 18g|Protein: 40g|Fiber: 1g

INGREDIENTS:

1. Melted unsalted butter (½ cup)
2. Minced garlic (5 cloves)
3. Lemon rings (10 slices)
4. Raw honey (3 tablespoons)
5. Salmon fillet (1.75 pounds)
6. Kosher salt (1 teaspoon)
7. Fresh lemon juice (3 tablespoons)
8. Chopped fresh parsley (2 teaspoons)
9. Black pepper powder (1.2 teaspoon)

INSTRUCTIONS:

1. Prepare oven by preheating to 375°F.
2. Line a sheet pan with aluminium foil and place salmon, skin-side down, on it. Lift the edges of the foil so the buttery mixture won't spill out. We're getting to the buttery mixture part.
3. Tuck the lemon slices underneath the salmon all around with enough space in between them. Leave it alone for now.
4. Get a microwave safe bowl, scoop butter into it and warm until it completely melts. Doesn't take longer than 2 minutes.
5. Pour in lemon juice, garlic and honey. Mix thoroughly and drizzle this mixture all over the salmon leaving just a bit left.
6. Sprinkle salt and pepper over the salmon to season.
7. Close the foil. If it doesn't seal up completely, add another foil on top of it to get that done. It must be airtight so be sure to pinch the sides.
8. If you're not in a hurry, you can leave it to sit for about 15 minutes so the salmon will absorb the juices. Or you can just skip this because it'll turn out great either way.
9. Slide the sheet pan into the oven and cook for 17 minutes or so.
10. Take out the sheet pan and open up the foil packet to let the salmon breathe. Keep the sides lifted or the butter my mixture will spill out.
11. Increase the heat of the oven.
12. Drizzle some more buttery mixture over the salmon if you like taking into consideration the current amount of juices on the foil. You don't want too much because it will spill and get all over the place. If you choose not to use it right now, you can use it as finishing right before you serve.
13. Let the salmon bake for 10 minutes or more to get it golden as you'd like.
14. Sprinkle parsley if you like or just drizzle extra buttery mixture if you have any left.
15. Serve warm.

Classic Garlic-Baked Chicken Thighs

- Prep time: 10 minutes
- Cooking time: 20 minutes
- Serving: 4
- Calories: 550 kcal
- Fat: 42g|Carbs: 0g|Protein: 40g|Fiber: 0g

INGREDIENTS:

1. Pepper (4 teaspoon)
2. Garlic powder (½ teaspoon)
3. Salt (½ teaspoon)
4. Extra virgin olive oil (2 tablespoons)
5. Chicken thighs (4 large sizes)
6. Vegetable oil cooking spray

INSTRUCTIONS:

1. Prepare oven by preheating to 425°F.
2. Get a sheet pan lined with aluminium spoil and then coated with cooking spray.
3. In a mixing bowl, add pepper, garlic powder, olive oil and salt. Mix thoroughly.
4. Throw the chicken into the bowl and toss until it is completely coated in the flavored olive oil.
5. Arrange seasoned chicken thighs on the sheet pan making sure to spread them out for even cooking.
6. Slide the pan into the oven and roast for about 20 minutes or more if the chicken isn't cooked through.
7. Take the pan out of the oven and let it sit for 5 minutes.
8. Serve warm.

Chapter Four: Sheet Pan Dinner Recipes

The one thing most people look forward to after a long day in the outside world is a warm meal, which isn't usually attainable because of time and current energy level. I used to do a lot of takeout and pizza on weeknights, but guess who has been cured? I discovered the sheet pan and I can say for a fact that I eat full tasty meals every night now.

Many sheet pan meals take only a few minutes of preparation time so you can drop it in the oven and go have that much needed shower. This is a one pan meal so cleanup is going to be a total breeze. Believe me, a sink full of dirty pots and saucepans is not how you want to end your day. Let's take a look, shall we?

Smoky Roasted Chicken Breasts with Chickpeas, Tomatoes and Cilantro

- Prep time: 10 minutes
- Cooking time: 30 minutes
- Serving: 6
- Calories: 630kcal
- Fat: 26.5g|Protein: 50.7g|Carbs: 49g|Fiber: 13.9g

INGREDIENTS:

1. Minced garlic (4 cloves)
2. Sweet paprika (q teaspoon)
3. Salt (2 teaspoons)
4. Smoked paprika (1 tablespoon)
5. Extra virgin olive oil (5 tablespoons)
6. Crushed red pepper (½ teaspoon)
7. Whole milk Greek yogurt (1 cup)
8. Ground cumin (1 teaspoon)
9. Black pepper powder (1 teaspoon)

10. Drained and rinsed chickpeas (1 can)
11. Boneless chicken breasts with skin still intact (4 large sizes)
12. Fresh cilantro sprigs or Italian parsley (1 cup)
13. Grape tomatoes (2 cups)

INSTRUCTIONS:

1. Set your oven to 450°F.
2. Get a small bowl and in it, you're going to mix paprika, oil, crushed red pepper, cumin, garlic, a tablespoon of salt and pepper. Set aside.
3. Pour a tablespoon of olive oil in a different bowl and stir in the yogurt. Mix thoroughly and then set aside.
4. Arrange chicken on a sheet pan with the skin side facing up. Glaze the body and insides with 2 tablespoons of olive oil. Set aside.
5. Mix chickpeas, ½ of cilantro and tomatoes in a medium size bowl. Drizzle in the last tablespoon of oil and toss to mix.
6. Pour that mixture all around the chicken and use any extra oil left in the bowl to coat the chicken a bit more. Keep the skin side up because that's where the real roasting will happen.
7. Season with a teaspoon of salt and slide sheet pan into the oven to bake for about 30 minutes or until the chicken is thoroughly cooked.
8. Take the sheet pan out of the oven and serve the chicken on a plate. Pour beans, cilantro and tomatoes all over.
9. Drizzle yogurt sauce over it and serve.

Hearty Ratatouille with Goat's Cheese

- Prep time: 15 minutes
- Cooking time: 50 minutes
- Serving: 4
- Calories: 376kcal
- Fat: 16g|Protein: 14.3g|Carbs: 44g|Fiber: 11g

INGREDIENTS:

1. Tomato puree (1 can)
2. Red bell pepper (1 large)
3. Olive oil cooking spray
4. Sliced garlic (3 cloves)
5. Zucchini (1 large size)
6. Chopped yellow onion (½ medium size)
7. Chinese eggplant (1 large size)
8. Yellow squash (1 large size)
9. Freshly chopped thyme (1 teaspoon)
10. Kosher salt
11. Unpeeled Yukon gold potatoes (4 small sizes)
12. Black pepper powder
13. Extra virgin olive oil (2 tablespoons)
14. Cubed unsalted butter (2 tablespoons)

15. Soft goat cheese (4 oz)
16. Crusty bread
17. Freshly chopped basil leaves (1 tablespoon)

INSTRUCTIONS:

1. Set your oven to 375°F and place a rack about 3 or 4 inches away from the broiler and another rack at the center.
2. Coat a sheet pan with some cooking spray.
3. Scoop the tomato puree into the greased pan and throw in your onions and garlic. Now sprinkle a bit of salt and pepper and just spread it out on the pan using a spatula. Preferably a rubber one.
4. Sprinkle the butter cubes over that.
5. Remove the head of the pepper
6. Take out the seeds and using a sharp knife, cut a quarter inch rounds and cut each round into another quarter inch. Set aside.
7. Cut off the rough ends of the zucchini, squash and eggplant. Cut each of them into a quarter inch. Set aside.
8. Slice the potatoes into a quarter inch and layer them over the tomato base. Place the zucchini, squash and eggplant over this and season with thyme, salt, pepper and olive oil.
9. Slide the pan into the oven, place on the center rack and bake for 40 minutes or extra if the veggies aren't tender enough and the tomato puree isn't bubbling.
10. Take the pan out of the oven and increase the heat.
11. Crumble the goat cheese and sprinkle them evenly over the vegetables.
12. Put the pan back in the oven and broil for a minute to melt the cheese.
13. Serve with a sprinkle of chopped basil and crusty bread.

Sheet Pan Parmesan Crusted Salmon Wi

- Prep time: 5 minutes
- Cooking time: 20 minutes
- Serving: 4
- Calories: 505kcal per serving
- Fat: 48g|Protein: 41g|Carbs: 15g|Fiber: 4g

INGREDIENTS:

Broccoli

1. Extra virgin olive oil (2 ½ tablespoons)
2. Broccoli with the stems removed and set aside. Chopped florets (1 ¼ lbs.)
3. Minced garlic (1 clove)
4. Black pepper powder
5. Salt to taste

on

1. Minced garlic (1 clove)
2. Salmon fillets, skinless (4 large sizes)
3. Black pepper powder
4. Freshly chopped parsley (1 tablespoon)
5. Fresh lemon juice from zested lemon (1½ teaspoon)
6. Bread crumbs (¼ cup)
7. Lemon zest (1½ teaspoon)
8. Extra virgin olive oil (1½ tablespoons)
9. Salt
10. Shredded parmesan cheese (¼ cup)
11. Dried thyme (¼ teaspoon)
12. Mayonnaise (1½ tablespoons)

INSTRUCTIONS:

1. Get your oven ready. Set it to 400°F.
2. Coat a rimmed sheet pan with aluminium foil and nonstick cooking spray.
3. Arrange broccoli at the center of the sheet pan and season with a drizzle or olive oil and a sprinkle of garlic. Toss gently to mix.
4. Sprinkle salt and pepper then spread the broccoli to form a single layer but leave enough room in the middle for the salmon fillets.
5. Sprinkle the bottom of the salmon with salt and pepper before placing it on the sheet pan, in the center of the broccoli. Please leave about ¾ inches in between the salmon for even cooking. Set aside.
6. Mix garlic, mayonnaise and lemon juice in a small mixing bowl. Glaze about half a tablespoon of it on each salmon and sprinkle with salt and pepper. Again.
7. In a different mixing bowl, pour the breadcrumbs, lemon zest, parmesan, thyme, parsley and 1½ tablespoons of olive oil then mix thoroughly with a fork until incorporated.
8. Layer this mixture over the salmon and finally place the pan in the oven to bake for 15 minutes or so. The fillets should be thoroughly cooked through and golden.

One Pan Chicken Parmesan And Roasted Zucchini

- Prep time: 15 minutes
- Cooking time: 27 minutes
- Serving: 4
- Calories: 551kcal
- Fat: 20.1g|Protein: 66.8g|Carbs: 26.1g|Fiber: 3.6g

INGREDIENTS:

1. Italian seasoned panko bread crumbs (¾ cup)
2. Extra virgin olive oil (2 tablespoons)
3. Halved boneless chicken breast with the skin removed (4 medium sizes)
4. Marinara sauce (⅔ cup)
5. Shredded parmesan cheese (¼ cup)
6. Salt
7. Whole egg (1 large size)

8. Grated mozzarella cheese (⅔ cup)
9. Freshly chopped basil leaves (This is optional)
10. Black pepper powder
11. Garlic powder (½ teaspoon)
12. Chopped then sliced zucchini (1¼ lbs.)

INSTRUCTIONS:

1. Prepare your oven. Set it to 450°F.
2. Grease a rimmed sheet pan with nonstick cooking spray.
3. Put the parmesan cheese and panko breadcrumbs in a large Ziplock bag. Sprinkle a bit of pepper and salt before sealing it. Shake and squeeze the mag then open it and drizzle one tablespoon of olive oil in it. Zip it up again and shake to mix. Squeeze it a bit to get the olive oil into the mixture. Set aside.
4. Whisk eggs in a small mixing bowl. Dip the chicken in the bowl one at a time to coat then dip in the breadcrumbs mixture. Place the chicken at the center of the sheet pan and repeat the process with every piece of chicken you'll be using.
5. Place the pan in the oven and cook for 15 minutes.
6. Put zucchini in a large Ziplock bag. Drizzle olive oil over it and season with salt, garlic powder and pepper. Zip up the bag and squeeze to coat the zucchini in seasoning. Do this a few minutes to the end of the chicken cooking time so it will be ready for the next step.
7. Take the pan out of the oven and arrange zucchini all around the chicken in a single layer. Put the pan back into the oven and cook for an extra 10 minutes or longer if you're using really thick chicken breasts.
8. It's ready. Take it out of the oven and drizzle marinara sauce over the top of the chicken breasts. Layer mozzarella over the sauce and put the oven rack close to the broiler section.
9. Broil for about 2 minutes or until the cheese is completely melted.
10. Serve warm with basil sprinkles.

Sheet Pan Steak And Veggies

- Prep time: 15 minutes
- Cooking time: 15 minutes
- Serving: 6
- Calories: 480kcal
- Fat: 24g|Protein:36g|Carbs: 30g|Fiber: 5g

INGREDIENTS:

1. Minced garlic (3 cloves)
2. Baby red potatoes (2 pounds)
3. Dried thyme (1 teaspoon)
4. Dry top sirloin steak (2 pounds)
5. Extra virgin olive oil (2 tablespoons)
6. Kosher salt
7. Broccoli florets (16 ounces)
8. Black pepper powder

INSTRUCTIONS:

1. Set oven to 350°F.
2. Grease a sheet pan with a bit of cooking spray.
3. Set a pot of water on medium heat, add salt and potatoes. Cook for 15 minutes so it becomes parboiled. Now drain it and set aside.
4. Arrange broccoli on the greased sheet pan in an even layer. Do they say to the potatoes. Season with salt, garlic, pepper and thyme. Drizzle a bit of olive oil over that and gently toss to coat. You want everything properly seasoned.
5. Sprinkle salt and pepper over the steaks to season them. Place them on the same sheet pan in an even layer and slide pan into the oven to bake.
6. This should bake until the meat is browned and slightly burnt at the edges. If you enjoy medium rare, let it cook for only 5 minutes before you flip to the other side so 10 minutes in total.
7. Take out of oven and serve warm.
8. Top with garlic butter if you like

Sheet Pan Shrimp Boil

- Prep time: 5 minutes
- Cooking time: 27 minutes
- Serving: 4
- Calories: 30kcal
- Fat: 2.5g|Protein: 1g|Carbs: 2g|Fiber: 5g

INGREDIENTS:

1. Melted unsalted butter (¼ cup)
2. Old bay seasoning (1 tablespoon)
3. Lemon wedges (1 medium size)
4. Baby Dutch yellow potatoes (1 pound)
5. Minced garlic (4 cloves)
6. Freshly chopped parsley (2 tablespoons)
7. Sliced smoked andouille sausage (1 package)
8. Cut corn ears (6 pieces)
9. Peeled veinless shrimp (1 pound)

INSTRUCTIONS:

1. First things first, set your oven to 400°F.
2. Lightly grease a sheet pan with nonstick vegetable oil cooking spray. Set aside.
3. Put a pot of salted water over medium heat and pour in washed potatoes. Let it cook for 13 minutes or until it's a bit tender.
4. Add the corn 5 minutes to the end of cooking then drain excess water.
5. Mix garlic, old bay seasoning and butter in a tiny bowl.
6. Pour shrimp, potatoes, sausages and corn onto the sheet pan and spread them out.
7. Scoop butter mixture onto the pan and toss gently so you don't break up the potatoes. Make sure everything is coated is coated in butter mixture before you slide sheet pan into the oven to bake.
8. Leave to bake for 15 minutes or more if the corn isn't tender enough or the shrimp doesn't look opaque.
9. Serve warm with parsley toppings and lemon wedges.

Ranch Pork Chops And Potatoes Sheet Pan Dinner

- Prep time: 5 minutes
- Cooking time: 30 minutes
- Serving: 6
- Calories: 540kcal
- Fat: 20g|Protein: 55g|Carbs: 37|Fiber: 5g

INGREDIENTS:

1. Smoked paprika (1 teaspoon)
2. Black pepper powder (1 teaspoon)
3. Extra virgin olive oil (3 tablespoons)
4. Dried oregano (1 tablespoon)
5. Baby potatoes (2lb)
6. Ranch salad dressing and seasoning mix (1 oz)
7. Freshly chopped parsley (1 tablespoon)
8. Boneless pork chops (6 medium sizes)

INSTRUCTIONS:

1. Prepare your oven. Set it to 400°F.
2. Lightly grease a sheet pan with cooking spray.
3. Arrange potatoes and pork chops on the sheet pan and pour olive oil all over them. Use a spatula to toss so the oil get everywhere. Set aside
4. Get a tiny mixing bowl and pour in smoked paprika, black pepper, ranch seasoning and oregano. Mix thoroughly then pour all over greased potatoes and pork chops. Use clean to coat the potatoes and pork chops in the oregano mixture.
5. Season with salt if you like.
6. Slide the sheet pan into the oven and bake for 30 minutes or extra if the pork chops aren't cooked through and the potatoes are tender enough to be pierced by a fork. The timing isn't an exact science because there are different kinds of ovens, so go with the timing that works best for you.
7. Serve warm with a sprinkle of parsley.

Chapter Five: Sheet Pan Poultry Recipes

You cannot say sheet pan without talking about poultry. These guys own the game and they have been serving hot and tasty goodness since day one. A lot of sheet pan recipes are centered around poultry and for good reason. It is filling, versatile and plain yummy. If you're a vegan and you can't relate, don't worry, I have a little something for you too. However, if you're a chicken lover, this one's for you!

Hoisin Sriracha Sheet pan Chicken

- Prep time: 20 minutes
- Cooking time: 40 minutes
- Serving: 4
- Calories: 490kcal
- Fat: 24g|Protein: 28g|Carbs: 40g|Fiber: 5g

INGREDIENTS:

1. Maple syrup (2 tablespoons)
2. Minced garlic (2 cloves)
3. Hoisin sauce (⅓ cup)
4. Chicken thighs with the bones intact (4 medium sizes)
5. Low sodium soy sauce (⅓ cup)
6. Pepper (¼ teaspoon)
7. Rice vinegar (1 tablespoon)
8. Freshly minced ginger (½ teaspoon)
9. Extra virgin olive oil (2 tablespoons)

10. Sriracha chili sauce (2 tablespoons)
11. Cauliflower florets (4 cups)
12. Sesame oil (2 teaspoons)
13. Salt (¼ teaspoon)
14. Sweet red pepper (1 medium size)
15. Diced sweet potato (1 medium size)
16. Sesame seeds (This is optional)

INSTRUCTIONS:

1. Set oven to 400°F.
2. Line a sheet pan with aluminium foil and set aside.
3. In a medium mixing bowl, mix hoisin sauce, low sodium soy sauce, sesame oil, Sriracha chili sauce, minced garlic, maple syrup, minced fresh ginger root and rice vinegar. Set it aside.
4. Season the chicken with salt and pepper on both sides.
5. Put potatoes and chicken thighs on the sheet pan. Pour a tablespoon of olive oil followed by ⅓ hoisin mixture. Use clean hands to coat.
6. Slide the pan into the oven and bake for about 15 minutes. Flip chicken thighs and potatoes then add cauliflower, remaining olive oil, red pepper and ⅓ hoisin mixture.
7. Bake for an extra 25 minutes.
8. Serve warm with leftover hoisin sauce and sesame seeds.

Pan-Roasted Chicken and Vegetables

- Prep time: 15 minutes
- Cooking time: 45 minutes
- Serving: 6
- Calories: 345kcal
- Fat: 12g|Protein: 28g|Carbs: 31g|Fiber: 5g

INGREDIENTS:

1. Roughly chopped onion (1 large size)
2. Minced garlic (3 cloves)
3. Paprika (½ teaspoon)
4. Extra virgin olive oil (2 tablespoons)
5. Fresh baby spinach (6 cups)
6. Cut red potatoes (6 medium)
7. Salt (1 ¼ teaspoons)
8. Black pepper powder (¾ teaspoon)
9. Skinless chicken thighs with the bones intact (6 medium sizes)
10. Dried crushed rosemary (1 teaspoon)

INSTRUCTIONS:

1. Prepare the oven. Set it to 425°F.
2. Mix onion, ¾ teaspoon of salt, oil, ½ teaspoon of rosemary, ½ teaspoon of pepper, garlic and potatoes in a medium sized mixing bowl.
3. Grease a sheet pan with cooking spray and pour in seasoned potatoes. Set aside.
4. Get a much smaller bowl and mix the remaining salt, pepper, rosemary and paprika. Coat chicken in paprika mixture and place over the veggies.
5. Slide sheet pan in the oven and bake for 40 minutes or extra if the veggies aren't tender enough.
6. Take the sheet pan out of the oven and transfer the chicken to a plate to cool.
7. Place spinach on top of the veggies still on the sheet pan and bake for 10 minutes.
8. Stir veggies to mix and serve warm with chicken.

Balsamic Roasted Chicken Thighs with Root Vegetables

- Prep time: 15 minutes
- Cooking time: 35 minutes
- Serving: 6
- Calories: 480kcal per serving
- Fat: 27g|Protein: 27g|Carbs: 33g|Fiber: 5g

INGREDIENTS:

1. Balsamic vinaigrette (2 tablespoons)
2. Extra virgin olive oil (4 tablespoons)
3. Chicken thighs (6 medium sizes)
4. Stone-ground mustard (3 tablespoons)
5. Diced peeled parsnips (4 medium sizes)
6. Kosher salt (¾ teaspoon)
7. Peeled and diced sweet potato (1 medium size)
8. Black pepper powder (¾ teaspoon)

9. Caraway seeds (¼ teaspoon)
10. Crumbled cooked bacon (3 strips)
11. Chopped shallots (4 medium sizes)
12. Fresh minced parsley (4 tablespoons)

INSTRUCTIONS:

1. Mix mustard, half a teaspoon of pepper, 3 tablespoons of oil, vinaigrette and half a teaspoon of salt in a large mixing bowl.
2. Throw in chicken and toss to coat.
3. Cover the bowl and place it in the fridge overnight or at least 6 hours.
4. Set your oven to 425°F.
5. Grease a sheet pan and arrange chicken on one side with the skin side facing up.
6. Pour sweet potato cubes and parsnips, caraway seeds, shallot, leftover pepper, oil and salt in a bowl. Mix thoroughly to coat
7. Pour potato mixture onto the other side of the pan and spread them out to form an even layer.
8. Slide the pan into the oven and bake for 20 minutes. Stir veggies and roast again for an additional 20 minutes or more to get the veggies really tender.
9. Pour vegetables in a bowl and sprinkle with half of the bacon and about 2 tablespoons of parsley. Sprinkle the rest over the chicken and serve together.
10. Bon appétit!

Spatchcock Chicken, Hasselback Potato, and Zucchini Fries

- Prep time: 25 minutes
- Cooking time: 1 hour 5 minutes
- Serving: 4
- Calories: 543kcal
- Fat: 17g|Protein: 42g|Carbs: 55g|Fiber: 6g

INGREDIENT:

1. Kosher salt (1 ¼ teaspoons)
2. Cooking spray
3. Finely chopped rosemary (1 ½ tablespoons)
4. Black pepper powder (1 teaspoon)
5. Russet potatoes (4 medium sizes)
6. Cornmeal (⅓ cup)
7. Lemon zest (1 tablespoon)
8. Grated garlic (2 cloves)
9. Whole chicken (1 medium size)
10. Extra virgin olive oil (2 tablespoons)
11. Garlic powder (1 teaspoon)
12. Zucchini (1 pound)
13. Smoked paprika (½ teaspoon)
14. Cornstarch (2 tablespoons)

INSTRUCTIONS:

1. Get your oven ready. Preheat to 450°F.
2. In a small mixing bowl, pour in lemon zest, garlic, half a spoon of salt and pepper and all the rosemary. Mix thoroughly and set aside.
3. Put the chicken on a chopping board and remove the backbone using kitchen scissors. How to? Place the breast side on the chopping board and cut along the edges of the back bone. Once that's put, throw it away. We won't need it.
4. Flip the chicken so the breast side is facing up. Use clean hands to press against the breast bone so the chicken splays open looking like a really large butterfly. Get rid of any excess fat and tuck the tip of the wings under the bird.
5. Grease a sheet pan and place the chicken right at the center.
6. Put your fingers under the skin (you can start anywhere) and apply spice mixture to the meat under the skin. It doesn't matter where you start, just make sure you season every inch of meat of your bird. Set aside.
7. You're going to cut through your potatoes now. Not all the way through, however. Do this from one end to the other.
8. Place potatoes very gently around the chicken and glaze with a tablespoon of olive oil.
9. Slide the pan into the oven and cook for 45 minutes.
10. While that is happening, you'll have time to make the zoodles. Shred the zucchini into noodles using a spiralizer. Use paper towels to remove excess moisture. You can also slice the zoodles into much shorter lengths if you like.
11. Mix cornstarch, paprika, cornmeal and garlic powder in a medium sized bowl. Pour in zoodles and toss.
12. Take the pan out of the oven and return chicken to the chopping board. Use paper towels to remove any chicken juice left in the center of the pan and replace that with cooking spray.
13. Pour leftover olive oil over the potatoes and spread the zoodles all around them. Slide the pan back into the oven and cook for 15 minutes. The potatoes should be cooked through and tender, the same goes for the zucchini.
14. Season both of them with the remaining salt and half a teaspoon of pepper. Skin the chicken and serve warm.

Chapter Six: Sheet Pan Seafood Recipes

If you're an avid practitioner of meatless Mondays, you'll understand when I tell you that they are much easier to get through when you have a large collection of tasty seafood recipes up your sleeve. If you're trying to cut back on your meat consumption of you just love the taste of seafood yumminess, I got you covered. What's more? We get to do this, seafood style!

One Pan Lemon Salmon, Roasted Potato Parmesan Asparagus

- Prep time: 10 minutes
- Cooking time: 30 minutes
- Serving: 4
- Calories: 700kcal
- Fat: 50g|Protein: 32g|Carbs: 30g|Fiber: 6g

INGREDIENTS:

1. Salmon with the skin intact (1 pound)
2. Small baby potatoes (1 pound)
3. Raw honey (1 tablespoon)
4. Smoked paprika (2 teaspoons)
5. Extra virgin olive oil (¼ cup)
6. Cayenne pepper (¼ teaspoon)
7. Salt
8. Black pepper powder
9. Minced garlic (2 cloves)
10. Lemon zests (2 medium sized lemons)
11. Sliced lemon (1 medium size)

Dried parsley (1 tablespoon)
13. Dried oregano (1 tablespoon)
14. Dried thyme (1 tablespoon)
15. Asparagus with the ends removed (1 bunch)
16. Chopped fresh basil leaves (½ cup)
17. Freshly shredded parmesan cheese (½ cup)

Basil Chimichurri:

1. Red wine vinegar (2 tablespoons)
2. Fresh cilantro (½ cup)
3. Ground red pepper (¼ teaspoon)
4. Extra virgin olive oil (⅓ cup)
5. Fresh basil leaves (1 cup)
6. Garlic (1 clove)
7. Salt

INSTRUCTIONS:

1. Prepare your oven by setting it to 425°F.
2. Place potatoes on a large sheet pan and drizzle 2 tablespoons of olive oil over them. Now sprinkle salt and pepper then toss to get every inch of the potatoes coated in seasoning.
3. Slide sheet pan into the oven and bake for 15 minutes.
4. While that is going on, get a small bowl and mix another 2 tablespoons of olive oil, thyme, garlic, raw honey, cayenne, oregano, parsley, lemon zest, paprika and basil. Set aside and wait for 15 minutes to be up.
5. Check on your potatoes, it should be 15 minutes now. Take them out of the oven, place salmon in the center of the pan and glaze salmon with the oregano mixture. Make sure the seasoning gets everywhere, you don't want uneven flavoring.
6. Now place the asparagus on the pan and toss to mix with the roasted potatoes.
7. Pour shredded parmesan cheese over that mixture and throw lemon slices all around the sheet pan.
8. Slide the pan into the oven and cook for about 20 minutes or until salmon is completely cooked through.
9. Take the pan out of the oven and remove the salmon skin. Slice into 4 pieces and serve with asparagus, potatoes and basil chimichurri. We're getting to that.

Basil Chimichurri:

1. Put all the ingredients in a food processor and blitz until it is one big mix.
2. Transfer into to glass jar or something.

Sheet Pan Lemon and Herb Cod with Vegetables

- Prep time: 10 minutes
- Cooking time: 25 minutes
- Serving: 4
- Calories: 195kcal
- Fat: 0.9g|Protein: 31g|Carbs: 15g|Fiber: 5.7g

INGREDIENTS:

1. Sliced yellow onion (1 medium size)
2. Fine sea salt (2 teaspoons)
3. Washed and picked parsley (½ cup)
4. Washed dill (¼ cup)
5. Avocado oil (4 teaspoons)
6. Washed green beans with trimmed edges (1lb)
7. Washed and picked cilantro (½ cup)
8. Lemon zest (2 teaspoons)
9. Wild caught cod(2ln sliced into 4 pieces)
10. Black pepper powder (1 teaspoon)
11. Fresh lemon juice) 2 teaspoons)
12. Scallion (1)
13. Diced zucchini (1 large size)
14. Garlic (8 cloves)
15. Lemon slices

INSTRUCTIONS:

1. Set your oven to 400°F.
2. Place green beans, 6 cloves of garlic and onions on a sheet pan. Drizzle 2 teaspoons of avocado oil and sprinkle with half a teaspoon of pepper and a teaspoon of salt. Toss to mix.
3. Slide the pan into the oven and bake for 10 minutes.
4. While that is going on, you should make the lemon in herb sauce. Bring out a blender, pour in lemon zest, 2 cloves of garlic, cilantro, scallion, lemon juice, dill, parsley and a quarter teaspoon each of salt and pepper. Put the lid on and blitz until thoroughly mixed. Set aside.
5. Take sheet pan out of the oven and add sliced zucchini to the mix. Pour in lemon juice mixture and toss to mix.
6. Make some space in the middle of the pan for the fish. Place fish in the fish spot and pour the remaining 2 teaspoons of oil, ½ teaspoon of black pepper and ¾ teaspoon of salt.
7. Slide pan back into the oven and bake again for 17 minutes.
8. Serve cooked fish and veggies with a drizzle of lemon herb sauce and lemon slice garnish.

Sheet Pan Clam Bake

- Prep time: 10 minutes
- Cooking time: 30 minutes
- Serving: 8
- Calories: 405kcal
- Fat: 22g|Protein: 29g|Carbs: 16g|Fiber: 0g

INGREDIENTS:

1. Melted unsalted butter (¼ cup)
2. Scrubbed littleneck clams (24)
3. Minced garlic (4 cloves)
4. Peeled, veinless shrimp (8 oz)
5. Baby Dutch yellow potatoes (1 pound)

bbed and debearded mussels (1 pound)

rn ears (6 pieces)

Old bay seasoning (1 tablespoon)

9. Sliced hot dried chorizo (1 pound)
10. Freshly chopped thyme leaves(1 tablespoon)
11. Red onion wedges (1 medium size)
12. Kosher salt
13. Black pepper powder
14. Halved lemons (2 medium sizes)
15. Freshly chopped chives (2 tablespoons)

INSTRUCTIONS:

1. Prepare your oven. Set it to 400°F.
2. Grease a sheet pan with the usual olive oil or nonstick cooking spray.
3. Put a pot of water over medium heat, sprinkle in a bit of salt and add the potatoes.
4. Let i5 cook for about 13 minutes or until it's a bit tender. Throw in the cut corn ears 5 minutes to the end of kitchen time.
5. When it's ready, drain and set aside.
6. Mix garlic, thyme, butter, old bay seasoning and pepper in a bowl.
7. Spread out the potatoes, clams, corn, shrimp, onion, mussels, lemons and chorizo on the sheet pan. Add butter mixture and carefully toss to mix.
8. Slide the pan into the oven and cook for 15 minutes or more of the clams and mussels haven't opened up and the shrimps are still not opaque.
9. Serve warm with chives garnish.

Parmesan Crusted Tilapia With Mayo

- Prep time: 5 minutes
- Cooking time: 10 minutes
- Serving: 6
- Calories: 186kcal
- Fat 14g|Protein: 15g|Carbs: 0.2g|Fiber: 0.1g

INGREDIENTS:

1. Garlic salt (1 ½ teaspoon)
2. Shredded parmesan cheese (6 tablespoons)
3. Tilapia fillets (6.5 ounces)
4. Black pepper powder (½ teaspoon). This is optional.
5. Lemon. This is optional.
6. Mayonnaise (¼ cup)
7. Soft low carb vegetables (For example, green beans, tomatoes, zucchini, etc.). This is optional.

INSTRUCTIONS:

1. Prepare your oven, set it to 400°F.
2. Prepare your sheet pan too. Line it with parchment paper or aluminium foil and spray either one with cooking spray.
3. Arrange the tilapia fillets on the sheet pan and season with black pepper and garlic salt. Flip and do the same to the other side.
4. Glaze each fillet with 2 teaspoons on mayonnaise and layer shredded parmesan cheese on top.
5. You can choose to place some soft low carb vegetables like bell peppers around the fillets in an even layer. Harder veggies won't work because the fish won't really give them time to cook through.
6. Pour olive oil, salt and pepper over them and put the pan in the oven to cook.
7. The cooking time depends on the fish, so you see why we used soft vegetables. 12 to 15 minutes tops.
8. Drizzle lemon juice over it and serve.

Sheet Pan Orange Chili Salmon

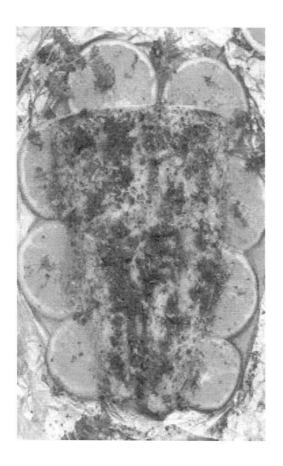

- Prep time: 5 minutes
- Cooking time: 25 minutes
- Serving: 3
- Calories: 960kcal
- Fat: 66g|Protein: 47g|Carbs: 42g|Fiber: 4g

INGREDIENTS:

1. Thinly sliced oranges (1 large size)
2. Raw honey (4 tablespoons)
3. Salmon fillet with skin intact (1 pound)

4. Fresh orange juice (4 tablespoons)
5. Salt (½ teaspoon)
6. Melted unsalted butter (½ cup)
7. McCormick Chili seasoning mix (2 teaspoons)
8. Black pepper powder (½ teaspoon)
9. Chopped fresh parsley leaves (1 tablespoon)

INSTRUCTIONS:

1. Prepare oven, preheat to 375°F.
2. Line a sheet pan with aluminium foil.
3. Put the salmon on the sheet pan with the flesh side up and raise the edges of the foil high enough for it not to spill the buttery mixture that we will soon be using.
4. Tuck orange slices beneath the fish with the same amount of space between them. Set aside.
5. Scoop the butter into a microwave safe bowl and heat on high for a minute or until the butter completely melts.
6. Whisk in orange juice and raw honey then drizzle a bit of the mixture over the salmon. Don't throw away the leftover, you'll need it.
7. Sprinkle McCormick chili seasoning mix, pepper and salt over the salmon and seal the foil with an extra piece of foil. Pinch the edges to make it as airtight as possible. If you're not in a hurry, you can enhance the flavour by leaving the pan alone for 15 minutes to marinade the salmon. It will taste great either way.
8. Slide pan into the oven to cook for 15 minutes.
9. Take the pan out of the oven and open up the top of the foil packet but leave the edges lifted because of the buttery mixture.
10. Raise the heat. Set to broil.
11. Drizzle the remaining buttery mixture over the salmon if you like. It's up to you, if you think there's already a lot of juice, you can save it for later.
12. Slide the pan into the oven and broil for roughly 10 minutes. Watch it very closely so it doesn't burn. The exact cooking time for this depends on the oven and salmon thickness so you're a little bit on your own here. All you need to know is that it should look golden-brown when it's ready and cooked through.
13. Garnish with parsley or buttery mixture and serve warm.

Pistachio Crusted Salmon With Glazed Carrots

- Prep time: 10 minutes
- Cooking time: 20 minutes
- Serving: 4
- Calories: 348kcal
- Fat: 20.3g|Protein: 25.4g|Carbs: 15g|Fiber: 1.5g

INGREDIENTS:

1. Extra virgin olive oil (¼ cup)
2. Minced ginger root (½ tablespoon)
3. Salmon fillets (3 pieces, 4 oz each)
4. Maple syrup (3 tablespoons)
5. Minced garlic (1 teaspoon)
6. Pepper
7. Shallot

8. Paprika or chili pepper powder (½ teaspoon)
9. Balsamic or apple cider vinegar (1 tablespoon)
10. Parsley
11. Baby carrots (1 lb.)
12. Sea salt
13. Ground pistachios (½ cup)
14. Lemon

INSTRUCTIONS:

1. Prepare your oven, set it to 400°F.
2. Wash the salmon, place it on a plate and put in the fridge until ready for use.
3. Mix olive oil, ginger, garlic, balsamic vinegar, spices, maple syrup, salt and pepper in a bowl.
4. Put the carrots on the sheet pan and glaze the top with the ginger mixture. Slide the pan in the oven to bake for 10 minutes.
5. Toss carrots with tongs and raise the temperature to 425°F.
6. Put the salmon and shallots in between the carrots. Place some lemon slices between the salmon and carrots. Drizzle lemon juice over them and season with salt and pepper.
7. Right before you return the pan to the oven, coat the salmon with the remaining garlic mixture.
8. Let it cook for 7 minutes.
9. Bring out the pan and coat the salmon with pistachios. Return to the oven and cook for an extra 3 minutes or more if the salmon isn't cooked through.
10. Sprinkle with fresh parsley and serve.

Sheet Pan Green Goddess Salmon With Bacony Brussels Sprouts

- Prep time: 10 minutes
- Cooking time: 13 minutes
- Serving: 4
- Calories: 250kcal
- Fat: 20g|Protein: 6g|Carbs: 12g|Fiber: 5g

INGREDIENTS:

1. Bacon (3 strips)
2. Kosher salt
3. Salmon fillets (4 center cut
4. Brussels sprouts (1lb)
5. Black pepper powder
6. Homemade basil green goddess dressing (3 tablespoons)
7. Extra virgin olive oil (2 tablespoons)
8. Kale microgreens (This is optional)
9. Parchment paper.

INSTRUCTIONS:

1. Prepare oven. Set to 400°F.
2. Line a sheet pan with parchment paper and place sliced brussels sprouts with the woody ends removed on it.
3. Chop the bacon into half inch chunks and place them on the sheet pan.
4. Drizzle 2 tablespoons of olive oil over the sprouts and bacon. Toss gently to coat. Sprinkle with pepper and salt. Toss again.
5. Slide the pan into the oven to roast for about 13 minutes.
6. While that is going on, season the salmon fillets with salt, pepper and olive oil.
7. The 13 minutes should be up at this point. Take out the sheet pan and make a circle in the bacon and brussels mixture. Place the salmon in the middle and return the pan to the oven to roast and an additional 15 minutes.
8. To serve, pour goddess sauce all over salmon fillets and garnish with kale microgreens (optional, of course).

Sheet Pan Blackened Salmon And Potato Bowl With Avocado Goddess Sauce

- Prep time: 15 minutes
- Cooking time: 40 minutes
- Serving: 6
- Calories:890kcal
- Fat: 50g|Protein: 39g|Carbs: 79g|Fiber: 14g

INGREDIENTS:

1. Extra virgin olive oil (¼ cup)
2. Raw honey (1 tablespoon)
3. Small baby potatoes (1 pound)
4. Smoked paprika (2 teaspoons)
5. Kosher salt
6. Cooked brown rice (3 cups)
7. Black pepper powder
8. Cumin (2 teaspoons)
9. Salmon fillets (4 large sizes)

10. Minced garlic (4 cloves)
11. Ground red pepper flakes (1 pinch)
12. Crumbled feta cheese (8 ounces)
13. Fresh lemon juice (2 medium sized lemons)

Avocado Goddess Sauce:

1. Fresh cilantro (1 cup)
2. Cumin (1 teaspoon)
3. Halved avocado (1 large size)
4. Fresh basil leaves (½ cup)
5. Fresh lemon juice (1 medium sized lemon)
6. Kosher salt
7. Halved seedless jalapeño
8. Plain Greek yogurt (¼ cup)

INSTRUCTIONS:

1. Prepare oven. Preheat to 425°F.
2. Place potatoes on a rimmed sheet pan and drizzle olive oil over them. Toss to coat.
3. Sprinkle black pepper and salt over the oiled potatoes and bake for 20 minutes.
4. Put the salmon on a plate and coat the top with honey. Sprinkle with cumin, garlic, salt, paprika, red pepper flakes and black pepper. Pour some lemon juice and olive oil over this.
5. Use clean hands to massage this into the fillets.
6. Take potatoes out of the oven and gently move them to one side of the pan to make space for the salmon.
7. Place the salmon on the sheet pan and put it back in the oven for an extra 20 minutes. The salmon should be cooked through if done right.
8. While the salmon is baking, go ahead to prepare the goddess sauce. Mix all the ingredients in a blender and blitz until you get a creamy smooth mixture. Add a bit of water to thin out the consistency if you like.
9. Spread the sauce on the plates and scoop some brown rice onto it. Place potatoes, salmon and feta over that and serve.
10. Top with fresh basil and lemon juice if you like.

Spring Salmon And Peas

- Prep time: 15 minutes
- Cooking time: 15 minutes
- Serving: 2
- Calories: 400kcal
- Fat: 17g|Protein: 25g|Carbs: 26g|Fiber:7g

INGREDIENTS:

Ginger Miso Marinade:

1. Mirin (¼ cup)
2. Extra virgin olive oil (1 tablespoon)
3. Sweetener (Maple syrup, brown sugar or raw honey)
4. Miso paste (2 tablespoons)
5. Toasted sesame oil (1 tablespoon)
6. Grated ginger (1 teaspoon)

Others:

1. Orange zest (1 teaspoon)
2. Snap peas or fresh snow (2 cups)
3. Black cod or sea bass salmon (6 ounces)
4. Sub frozen peas, fresh shelled spring peas or shelled edamame (1 cup)
5. Pepper
6. Salt

INSTRUCTIONS:

1. Prepare your oven, set it to 400°F.
2. Place a saucepan over low heat and pour in the marinade ingredients. Stir slowly and steadily until it's noticeably smooth. This really only helps the ingredients to mix properly.
3. Line a sheet pan with parchment paper and place the snap and spring peas on one side of it.
4. Use some paper towels to pat the salmon dry then generously coat it with miso marinade on both sides.
5. Sprinkle, salt, pepper and a bit of orange zest.
6. Pour the leftover marinade once the snap and spring peas. Toss to coat.
7. Slide the pan into the oven and bake for about 15 minutes. Note that thicker salmon cuts will take longer and thinner ones, shorter.
8. Top with scallions and sesame seeds.
9. Serve.

Chapter Seven: Sheet Pan Veggie Recipes

Chickens don't always have to be the star of sheet pan meals and no; I'm not headed towards the salmon. This one is all about the veggies. They are no longer sidekicks to the chicken, people! They have full recipes and I have come to appreciate the flavor they bring to the table... Quite literally, in fact. The most interesting part about this is how limitless it really is. You can mix just about any vegetables you like and voila! A whole meal.

Easy Oven-Roasted Vegetables

- Prep time: 10 minutes
- Cooking time: 30 minutes
- Serving: 4
- Calories: 120 kcal per serving
- Fat: 7g|Protein: 2g|Carbs: 13g|Fiber: 3g

INGREDIENTS:

1. Green bell pepper (1 medium size)
2. Salt (½ teaspoon)
3. Sweet potato (1 medium size)
4. Garlic powder (1 teaspoon)
5. Red bell pepper (1 medium size)
6. Extra virgin olive oil (2 tablespoons)
7. Red onion (1 medium size)

INSTRUCTIONS:

1. Prepare your oven. Set it to 425°F.
2. Get a parchment-lined sheet pan ready and set aside.
3. Cut the onion and peppers in half inch squares. While you cut the onions, you'll notice that some layers stick together even after you've sliced through, use your fingers to take them apart. Set aside.
4. Slice sweet potato into a quarter inch discs and dice each piece into an even smaller piece.
5. Get a fairly large mixing bowl, pour in salt, garlic powder and olive oil. Mix thoroughly.
6. Pour in the onions, sweet potatoes and peppers. Toss gently.
7. Now spread this out on a sheet pan in an even layer.
8. Slide the pan into the oven and let it bake for 30 minutes.
9. Take the sheet out of the oven, let it cool for a bit then serve!

Maple Cinnamon Roasted Butternut Squash

- Prep time: 10 minutes
- Cooking time: 40 minutes
- Serving: 4
- Calories: 67 kcal per serving
- Fat: 5g|Protein: 0g|Carbs: 5g|Fiber: 0g

INGREDIENTS:

1. Extra virgin olive oil (q ½ tablespoons)
2. Cinnamon powder (½ teaspoon)
3. Peeled, seedless, sliced butternut squash. (1 large size)
4. Maple syrup(1 ½ tablespoons)
5. Salt
6. Black pepper powder

INSTRUCTIONS:

1. First thing to do is preheat your oven. Set it to 400°F.

2. Prepare a sheet pan right after that with either spray or parchment paper.
3. Pour cubed butternut squash onto the sheet pan and spread it out evenly or not, it doesn't really matter. Layer on some olive oil and maple syrup then season salt, cinnamon powder and pepper. Use clean hands to coat the butternut cubes in seasoning
4. Slide the pan into the oven and vane for about 40 minutes or extra if the squash cubes aren't tender enough.
5. Take the pan out of the oven and leave to cool for a bit before serving.

Sheet Pan Honey Balsamic Chicken and Vegetables

- Prep time: 15 minutes
- Cooking time: 45 minutes
- Serving: 4
- Calories: 480 kcal
- Fat: 14g | Protein: 41g | Carbs: 53g | Fiber: 8g

INGREDIENTS:

1. Dijon mustard (1 teaspoon)
2. Chicken breasts (1½ pounds
3. Raw honey (6 tablespoons)
4. Dried thyme leaves (½ teaspoon)
5. Extra virgin olive oil (2 tablespoons)
6. Balsamic vinegar (4 tablespoons)

7. Cinnamon powder (¼ teaspoon)
8. Any mixed vegetables you like, e.g. bell peppers, broccoli, zucchini, cauliflower etc. (1 ½ pounds)
9. Black pepper powder
10. Salt (1½ teaspoons)

INSTRUCTIONS:

1. Inside a Ziplock bag, pour in honey, dried thyme, balsamic vinegar, a tiny pinch of cinnamon powder and Dijon mustard. Mix the ingredients inside the bag with a spatula. Or just zip it up and use your hands to mix it from the outside.
2. Get a sharp knife, slice through the chicken breasts in 2 inch pieces and sprinkle a teaspoon of black pepper and salt.
3. Open up your Ziplock bag and drop the chicken inside it. Zip it up and give the back a shake until all parts of the chicken have honey balsamic marinade. Place the bag in the fridge and leave it to marinade for 1 hour to 8 hours.
4. Get your oven ready, preheat to 400°F.
5. Prepare your sheet pan by lining with parchment paper. Set aside.
6. Slice the vegetables into even bits. Veggies like cauliflower and broccoli should be cut into florets. Carrots should be cut into a quarter inch. Butternut squash and zucchini should be sliced into pieces as thick as half an inch. Bell peppers and onions should not be cut into strips. And oh, halve the brussels sprouts.
7. Now, that's settled. Spread the veggies out on the sheet pan. Coat them with olive oil, black pepper and salt.
8. Use clean hands to mix the veggies with the seasoning so that it is evenly spread and no veggie is left without seasoning.
9. Slide the pan into the middle rack of the oven and cook for 10 minutes.
10. Create a space in the center of the vegetables for the chicken
11. Take The Ziplock back out of the fridge and transfer the chicken pieces onto the sheet pan. Save the excess marinade
12. Put the sheet back into the oven and roast for about 29 minutes.
13. Place a pan over medium heat and pour in saved marinade. Lower the heat and constantly stir the mixture and watch it thicken. This is usually takes 3 minutes.
14. Turn off the heat and serve chicken and vegetables with honey marinade drizzled all over it.

Easy Balsamic Roasted Vegetables

- Prep time: 15 minutes
- Cooking time: 40 minutes
- Serving: 4
- Calories: 130 kcal per serving
- Fat: 7g|Protein: 2g|Carbs: 14g|Fiber: 3g

INGREDIENTS:

1. Red and green bell peppers (1 medium sized each)
2. Salt (½ teaspoon)
3. Sweet potato (1 medium size)
4. Extra virgin olive oil (2 tablespoons)
5. Garlic (2 cloves)
6. Red onion (1 medium size)
7. Fresh rosemary leaves (1 teaspoon)
8. Balsamic vinegar (2 tablespoons)
9. Feta cheese (1 tablespoon)

INSTRUCTIONS:

1. Prepare your oven. Set it to 425°F.
2. Coat a sheet pan with parchment paper. Set aside.
3. Chop the onion and bell peppers into half inch squares. This is almost like the first recipe in this section. Almost.
4. Use your fingers to take apart the onion layers. Set aside.
5. Slice the potatoes into a quarter inch discs which you'll eventually cut into quarters.
6. Mince the garlic and chop the fresh rosemary leaves.
7. In a mixing bowl large enough to hold all the ingredients, mix the rosemary, olive oil, garlic, balsamic vinegar and salt.
8. Throw in the rest of the ingredients; peppers, sweet potatoes and onions. Use clean hands to coat the veggies in the olive oil mixture.
9. Spread the veggies onto the prepared sheet pan. Slide the pan into the oven and bake for 40 minutes.
10. Take out the pan and leave to cool for a few minutes.
11. Serve with crumbled feta cheese if you like.

One-Pan Garlic-Parmesan Asparagus

- Prep time: 10 minutes
- Cooking time: 12 minutes
- Serving: 4
- Calories: 80 kcal per serving
- Fat: 4.5g|Protein: 4g|Carbs: 8g|Fiber: 4g

INGREDIENTS:

1. Asparagus (1 ⅓ pounds)
2. Salt (½ teaspoon)
3. Garlic (2 cloves)
4. Shredded parmesan cheese (2 tablespoons)
5. Extra virgin olive oil (1 tablespoon)
6. Black pepper powder

INSTRUCTIONS:

1. Prepare your oven. Set it to 400°F.
2. Get a parchment-lined sheet pan ready. Set aside.
3. Mince the cloves of garlic.
4. Remove the ends of the asparagus and place them on the sheet pan.
5. Cost the asparagus in oil and season with salt, black pepper.
6. Slide the pan into the middle rack of the oven.
7. Let it cook for 12 minutes or until veggies are softened.
8. Take the pan out of the oven and leave to cool.
9. Serve warm with a sprinkle of parmesan cheese.

Balsamic Honey Roasted Vegetables

- Prep time: 10 minutes
- Cooking time: 45 minutes
- Serving: 6
- Calories: 120 kcal
- Fat: 5g|Protein: 2g|Carbs: 18g|Fiber: 3g

INGREDIENTS:

1. 10 cups of any veggies you like. In this recipe, I used broccoli, sweet potato, bell pepper, beets and mushrooms. 2 cups each of washed and chopped vegetables.
2. Balsamic vinegar(2 tablespoons)
3. Extra virgin olive oil (2 tablespoons)
4. Honey (2 tablespoons)
5. Black pepper powder
6. Sea salt (¼ teaspoon)

INSTRUCTIONS:

1. Get your oven ready. Preheat to 400°F.
2. Get a parchment-lined sheet pan ready too. If you don't have any parchment paper, you can use a baking mat.
3. Pour evenly chopped veggies onto the sheet pan. Coat with oil, pepper and salt.
4. Slide the pan into the oven and let it cook for 20 minutes.
5. Shake the pan a bit to mix and turn the vegetables then leave to cook for an additional 15 minutes.
6. If the veggies are not golden brown or soft enough to be pierced by a fork, leave them in the oven for a few extra minutes. If not, they're ready.
7. Pour honey and balsamic vinegar over the vegetables and put the pan back into the oven for 10 more minutes. This is to caramelize the honey.
8. Serve warm.

Roasted Vegetables with Easy Tahini-Miso Sauce

- Prep time: 10 minutes
- Cooking time: 25 minutes
- Serving: 4
- Calories: 220 kcal per serving
- Fat: 15g|Protein: 7g|Carbs: 19g|Fiber: 6g

INGREDIENTS:

1. White miso (2 tablespoons)
2. Lemon juice (2 tablespoons)
3. Canola oil (2 tablespoons)
4. Tahini (¼ cup)
5. Salt (¼ teaspoon)
6. White onion (½ medium size)
7. Warm water (½ cup)
8. Broccoli florets (4 cups)
9. Pepper
10. Garlic (4 cloves)
11. Cooking spray

12. Red bell pepper (1 medium size)

INSTRUCTIONS:

1. Get your oven ready. Preheat to 425°F.
2. Get some aluminium foil and line a pan with it. Grease the foil with some cooking spray and set it aside.
3. Cut the onion and peppers into half inch squares then use your fingers to take apart the onion layers.
4. Crush the garlic and throw it in a large mixing bowl. add canola oil and salt then mix thoroughly.
5. Pour broccoli florets, onion and red pepper into the bowl and toss with a spatula to coat all sides of the vegetables with the garlic mixture.
6. Spread the seasoned vegetables out on the sheet pan and slide the pan into the oven to cook for 25 minutes.
7. Meanwhile, you have some free time so why not make the tahini-miso sauce.
8. Mix miso, lemon juice, warm water and tahini in a tiny bowl. Sprinkle a but a pepper to season and mix thoroughly. That's it!
9. Take the sheet pan out of the oven leave the veggies on it to cool for a few minutes.
10. Serve on a plate with a drizzle of tahini-miso sauce.

Chapter Eight: Sheet Pan Sauce Recipes

Sheet Pan Roasted Vegetable Sauce with Gnocchi

- Prep time: 15 minutes
- Cooking time: 40 minutes
- Serving: 4
- Calories: 2473kcal
- Fat: 67g|Protein: 62g|Carbs: 407g|Fiber: 5g

INGREDIENTS:

1. Extra virgin olive oil (1 bottle)
2. Vegetable broth (3 cups)
3. Any mixed vegetables you like (4 cups)
4. Sliced baby bok with the stem removed (1 medium size)
5. Kosher salt

6. Gnocchi (8 ounces)
7. Basil pesto (3 tablespoons)

INSTRUCTIONS:

1. Prepare your oven. Set it to 425°F.
2. Line a rimmed sheet pan with either aluminium foil, parchment paper or a silicon mat.
3. Mix the chopped vegetables in a bowl with 1 tablespoon of olive oil and ¼ teaspoon of salt. Spread the seasoned veggies onto the pan in an even layer.
4. Slide the pan into the oven to cook for roughly 30 minutes. Softer veggies should look light brown at the edges.
5. Pour roasted veggies into a soup pot placed over medium heat. Stir in 3 cups of broth and wait for the mixture to simmer.
6. Now throw in gnocchi, they will float when they have been cooked through. Nice indicator, eh?
7. Lower heat and add 3 tablespoons of basil pesto and baby bok choy. Leave to cool until greens are a bit wilted, but still a vibrant green color.
8. Serve warm.

Sheet Pan Roasted Red Pepper Tomato Soup

- Prep time: 15 minutes
- Cooking time: 40 minutes
- Serving: 4
- Calories: 180kcal per serving
- Fat: 8g|Protein: 7g|Carbs: 20g|Fiber: 5g

INGREDIENTS:

1. Thin onion wedges (½ medium size)
2. Vegetable broth (2 cups)
3. Seeded and quarter red bell peppers (1 ¼ lb.)
4. Fresh basil, chopped (1 tablespoon)

5. Roughly chopped carrots (2 medium sizes)
6. Halved small tomatoes (16 ounces)
7. Kosher salt (½ teaspoon)

Paprika roux (This is optional)

1. Flour (1 tablespoon)
2. Vegetable broth (1 cup)
3. Kosher salt (½ teaspoon)
4. Avocado oil or olive oil or butter for non-vegans (2 tablespoons)
5. Smoked paprika (1/2 teaspoon)
6. Cashew, soy or almond milk (¼ cup)

INSTRUCTIONS:

1. Prepare oven. Set it to 450°F.
2. Get a rimmed sheet pan, line with parchment paper or aluminium foil.
3. Pour the veggies onto the sheet pan and spread them out into an even layer.
4. Slide the pan into the oven and cool for 20-40 minutes or extra if the pepper skins aren't even slightly charred.
5. Now take the pan out of the oven and leave it to cool for a few minutes.
6. Once cooled, skin the peppers. It doesn't have to be all the skin, just the bubbled-up charred ones.
7. Pour the vegetables into a food processor or blender along with the juices. Add basil leaves, ⅓ teaspoon of salt and all the vegetable broth. Blitz until it's really smooth. You should have about a quart of sauce.
8. **Paprika roux:** Place a soup pot over medium-low heat. Pour butter or oil in it and stir until it is completely melted.
9. Add paprika and flour. Stir constantly until you have a paste. Pour in cashew or soymilk at intervals, still stirring.
10. Add the broth and stir until you get a smooth and loose mixture.
11. Now you can finish the sauce with or without the paprika roux. Pour the sauce into the pot. If you're using roux, pour that as well. Now place the pot over medium heat and cook through.
12. Adjust seasoning and serve.

Roasted Scallion Salsa Verde

- Prep time: 5 minutes
- Cooking time: 10 minutes
- Serving: 4
- Calories: 90kcal
- Fat: 2g|Protein: 3g|Carbs: 18g|Fiber: 6g

INGREDIENTS:

1. Red wine vinegar (¼ cup)
2. Halved garlic (4 cloves)
3. Finely chopped shallots (½ cup)
4. Chopped light and dark green parts of scallions (2 ¾ cups)
5. Fresh lime juice (¼ cup)
6. Tender stems and leaves of fresh cilantros (1 bunch)
7. Drained capers (2 tablespoons)
8. Extra virgin olive oil (½ cup)
9. Tender stems and leaves of fresh flat leaf parsley (1 bunch)

INSTRUCTIONS:

1. Get your oven ready. Set it to 400°F.
2. Get a mixing bowl. Throw in shallots, pour in vinegar and lime juice then sprinkle with salt.
3. Pour mixture and garlic onto a rimmed sheet pan and drizzle oil all over it. Use a spatula to toss so that the scallions are thoroughly coated.
4. Place a foil over the sheet pan and slide it into the oven to cook for about 10 minutes.
5. Take it out of the oven and leave to cool for a bit. Now move it to a cutting board and get chopping.
6. Throw the parsley and cilantro into a blender and blitz until it's in a lot of tiny bits.
7. Now mix the capers, garlic, herbs and scallions with shallots.
8. Sprinkle a bit of salt and pepper then serve.

Roasted Parsnip Cream Sauce

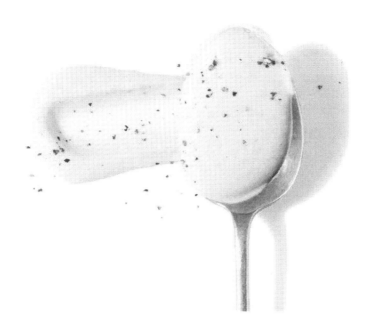

- Prep time: 5 minutes
- Cooking time: 25 minutes
- Serving: 2
- Calories: 207kcal per serving
- Fat: 7.5g|Protein: 2.8g|Carbs: 35.2g|Fiber: 7.9g

INGREDIENTS:

1. Smashed garlic (2 cloves)
2. Peeled parsnips chopped into 1 inch bits (2 cups)
3. Extra virgin olive oil (⅓ cup)
4. Hot water (½ cup)
5. Sour cream (¾ cup)
6. Sliced shallot (¼ cup)
7. Fresh lemon juice (3 tablespoons)

INSTRUCTIONS:

1. Get your oven ready. Heat to 425°F.
2. Mix shallots, garlic, parsnips and olive oil on a rimmed sheet pan. Sprinkle with pepper and salt then spread out the veggies into an even layer.
3. Slide the pan into the oven and cook for 25 minutes or extra if the parsnips aren't tender or a bit light brown.
4. Pour the roasted veggies plus juices into a food processor. Pour in lemon juice, half a cup of hot water and sour cream.
5. Blitz on high speed until it is pasty smooth. Add more water to thin the consistency if you like.
6. Adjust seasoning, blitz again to mix and serve.

Roasted Red Pepper And Tomato Sauce

- Prep time: 30 minutes
- Cooking time: 40 minutes
- Serving: 1 litre
- Calories: 180kccal
- Fat: 7g|Protein: 6g|Carbs: 20g|Fiber: 5g

INGREDIENTS:

1. Red peppers (2 medium sizes)
2. Sea salt (1¼ teaspoon)
3. Minced garlic (3 cloves)
4. Italian seasoning (1 teaspoon)

5. Black pepper (½ teaspoon)
6. Halved vine tomatoes (10 small sizes)
7. Extra olive oil (1 tablespoon)
8. Italian seasoning (1 teaspoon)

INSTRUCTIONS:

1. Prepare your oven, set it to 400°F.
2. Place your sheet pan on a work surface and place 2 whole red peppers without the stems and halved tomatoes with the flesh side down on it. Pour olive oil all over them and season with a quarter teaspoon of sea salt and garlic.
3. Slide the pan into the oven and cook for 40 minutes.
4. Take the pan out of the oven and place a large enough piece of foil over it to lock the steam in. Leave this on for 10 minutes. Take it off and leave it to cool for about 20 minutes.
5. Skin the red peppers and scrape out the seeds.
6. Transfer everything to a blender and blitz. Add seasoning; a teaspoon of sea salt, fresh basil, black pepper powder and Italian seasoning. Blitz again and again until you finally achieve the consistency you want.
7. Serve with noodles, pasta or any base you'd like.

Roasted Garlic Cream Sauce

- Prep time: 5 minutes
- Cooking time: 10 minutes
- Serving: 4
- Calories: 439kcal
- Fat: 14g|Protein: 7g|Carbs: 32.4g|Fiber: 5g

INGREDIENTS:

1. Heavy cream (1 ¾ cup)
2. Roasted garlic (1 head)

3. 1 tablespoon of heavy cream + 2 teaspoons flour
4. Butter (6 tablespoons)
5. Parmesan cheese (1 ¼ cup)
6. Black pepper powder /1/2 teaspoon)

INSTRUCTIONS:

1. Prepare oven, preheat to 425°F.
2. Wash a head of garlic and place it on a sheet pan with a drizzle of olive oil.
3. Slide the pan into the oven to cook for about 20 minutes.
4. Take the pan out of the oven and let it cool for a while.
5. Separate the cloves and remove the skins. Crush them with a fork and set aside.
6. Place butter in a pan set over medium heat and stir until it melts.
7. Stir in cream and crushed garlic and leave till it simmers.
8. Stir in parmesan cheese, black pepper powder and flour and cream mixture. Stir with a wooden spatula to get rid of lumps that may form. Stir continuously until the sauce looks thick enough. Takes about 10 minutes.
9. Serve as a side.

Chapter Nine: Sheet Pan Gluten-free Recipes

Sheet Pan Pesto Chicken And Veggies

- Prep time: 10 minutes + 6 hours for marinating.
- Cooking time: 20 minutes
- Serving: 4
- Calories: 756kcal
- Fat: 46g|Protein: 55g|Carbs: 27g|Fiber: 5g

INGREDIENTS:

Chicken:

1. White wine vinegar (3 tablespoons)
2. Black pepper powder
3. Skinned boneless chicken breasts (4 medium sizes)
4. Salt (1 teaspoon)
5. Pesto (1 cup)

Vegetables:

1. Garlic salt (1 ½ teaspoons)
2. Quartered baby red potatoes (1 pound)
3. Asparagus with the edges trimmed and the body sliced into 2 inch bits (1 pound)
4. Extra virgin olive oil (5 tablespoons)

INSTRUCTIONS:

1. Put the chicken breasts in a large Ziplock bag along with salt, pepper, white wine vinegar and pesto. Zip it up and shake & squeeze to mix the seasoning and chicken breasts.
2. Put the bag on a large enough plate or dish and place in the fridge to marinate for 6 to 12 hours. Feel free to squeeze the bag every now while it's marinating.
3. Move the oven rack to the center and get your oven heated at 400°F.
4. Take the chicken out of the fridge and leave it alone to get to room temp.
5. While that is happening, slice your potatoes into another large Ziplock bag. Pour in 3 tablespoons of olive oil and season with pepper and ¾ teaspoon of garlic salt. Shake and squeeze the bag until the potatoes are completely coated and seasoned.
6. Spread potatoes out on a sheet pan in a single layer. Slide the pan into the oven and cook for 20 minutes.
7. Remember the Ziplock bag you used for the potatoes? You're going to need that place the asparagus inside it and add the remaining olive oil. Season with pepper and ¾ teaspoon of garlic salt. Shake and squeeze the bag to coat and season the asparagus. Leave it alone.
8. 20 minutes should be up by now so take the pan out of the oven, flip the potatoes and move them to one side of the pan.
9. Drain the pesto from the chicken breasts so you don't have excess oil all over the place. However, you can leave a bit of it on top of the chicken if you like.
10. Arrange the chicken on unoccupied part of the pan. Place the pan back into the oven and leave for 15 minutes.
11. Now, move the chicken to the center of the sheet pan and pour asparagus on the other side. Let it cook for about 15 minutes. The asparagus and potatoes should be soft if done right.
12. Serve warm.

Grain Free King Ranch Chicken Flautas

- Prep time: 15 minutes
- Cooking time: 45 minutes
- Serving: 18
- Calories:
- Fat: 6.5g|Protein: 40.8g|Carbs: 28.7g|Fiber: 2.5g

INGREDIENTS:

1. Shredded cooked chicken breast (10 ounces)
2. Chopped cherry tomatoes (¼ cup)
3. 6 inch cassava tortillas (2 batches)
4. Full fat coconut milk (2 tablespoons)
5. Chopped green onions or chives (⅛ cup)

6. Kite Hill Dairy-free cream cheese (8 ounces)
7. Chopped fresh hatch chilies (¼ cup)
8. Salt
9. Creamy ranch dressing
10. Pepper
11. Primal palate taco seasoning (½ teaspoon)
12. Pico de Gallo & cilantro (for serving)

Quick note:

Fresh homemade tortillas are usually my go-to for this recipe because they are super flexible, easy to roll and they hold at the seams just fine. However, there's always the option of using a pre-made like the ones I listed above. The only difference is, they are noticeably bigger than the usual 6-inch ones made by yours truly. Don't worry, you'll just have to use more filling and get less flautas. I just thought I'd point it out.

INSTRUCTIONS:

1. Mix the shredded chicken, coconut milk, chives, DF cream cheese, chili's spices and tomatoes in a bowl. Mix thoroughly. Use a spatula or whatever mixing tool works for you.
2. Sprinkle salt and pepper. Mix again.
3. For the flautas, you will need only 2 tablespoons of filling if you're using the 6-inch homemade version like me. If not, you'll need an extra spoon or so.
4. Scoop the filling onto the tortilla and lengthen it out with your spoon into a skinny line. Wrap it up like a burrito or cigarette. Don't pack on a lot of filling because the flautas is more likely to break up during cooking if it's rolled only once because of excess filling. Little filling = more rolling = less breaking.
5. Arrange the flautas with the seam side facing down on the sheet pan. This is a crossroad. You can either go ahead and cook them or store them in the refrigerator for later. You cannot store them for any longer than a day. Also, premade tortillas usually require a toothpick to seal them until after cooking.
6. Preheat your oven to 350°F.
7. Slide the pan in it and leave to cook for about 45 minutes, flipping in between to ensure no side burns. When you're finished, take them out of the oven and set on a wire rack to cool.

8. To serve, place on flauta on a plate and pour enough creamy dressing over it. Garnish with cilantro or Pico de Gallo and a little extra ranch dressing if you like.

Creamy Ranch Dressing

INGREDIENTS:

1. Apple cider vinegar (1 teaspoon)
2. Your favourite mayonnaise (½ cup)
3. Dried chives (1 teaspoon)
4. Full fat coconut milk (1 tablespoon)
5. Garlic granules (¼ teaspoon)
6. Salt and pepper powder

INSTRUCTIONS:

1. Mix all the ingredients thoroughly in a tiny bowl. Use more coconut milk for a thinner consistency and mayonnaise for a thicker consistency.
2. Enjoy!

Easy Chicken Pita

- Prep time: 15 minutes
- Cooking time: 25 minutes
- Serving: 6
- Calories: 422kcal
- Fat: 10g|Protein: 28g|Carbs: 39g|Fiber: 3g

INGREDIENTS:

1. Diced red onion (1 medium size)
2. Skinned boneless chicken thighs (1lb)
3. Chopped artichoke hearts (1 can)
4. Halved cherry tomatoes (1 cup)
5. Extra virgin olive oil (1 tablespoon)
6. Diced red bell pepper (1 medium size)
7. Dried basil (2 teaspoon)
8. Halved pitted olives (½ cup)
9. Hummus (½ cup)

10. Red pepper flakes (2 teaspoons)
11. Whole white pitas (6 pieces)
12. Dried oregano (2 teaspoons)
13. Parsley
14. Cilantro
15. Salt
16. Black pepper powder

INGREDIENTS:

1. Put red bell pepper, artichoke hearts, tomatoes, olives and onions in a bowl. Drizzle with olive oil and season with salt and pepper. Toss to coat the veggies in the seasoning and transfer them to the sheet pan. Spread them out for even cooking.
2. Drop chicken thighs right on top of the vegetables and season with red pepper flakes, black pepper, oregano, salt and basil.
3. Slide the pan into the oven and cook for about 25 minutes. Ovens are different so you might need some extra time if your chicken isn't cooked through.
4. Use a sharp knife to cut the chicken into bits. Mix with the veggies.
5. Warm the pitas and spread some hummus on the inside. Stuff each pita with chicken and vegetables.
6. Serve with parsley or cilantro garnish.

Sheet Pan Balsamic Rosemary Potatoes with Mushrooms, White Beans and Kale

- Prep time: 15 minutes
- Cooking time: 45 minutes
- Serving: 4
- Calories: 490kcal
- Fat: 14g|Protein: 21g|Carbs: 70g|Fiber: 12g

INGREDIENTS:

1. High heat oil (2 tablespoons)
2. Balsamic vinegar (4 tablespoons)
3. Fingerling potatoes (2 pounds)
4. Freshly chopped rosemary leaves (1 tablespoon)

5. Low-sodium tamari (3 tablespoons)
6. Chopped cremini mushrooms (16 ounces)
7. Drained, rinsed white beans (1 can)
8. Tahini (2 tablespoons)
9. Chopped mustard greens or kale with the stems removed (1 bunch)
10. Olive oil (1 tablespoon)

INSTRUCTIONS:

1. Get your oven ready. Set it to 450°F.
2. Line a sheet pan with a silicone mat or parchment paper.
3. Place fingerling potatoes on the pan and coat with a tablespoon of high heat oil. Season with pepper & salt and slide the pan into the oven to cook for 45 minutes.
4. While the fingerlings are cooking, mix balsamic vinegar, tamari and another tablespoon of high heat oil in a medium sized bowl. Stir in 1 tablespoon of rosemary and throw in diced mushrooms. Stir until the mushrooms and thoroughly coated in seasoning. Leave it alone to marinate while the potatoes get ready.
5. Take the potatoes out of the oven, the potatoes should be cooked through now. Pour mushrooms without the marinade onto the pan. Do the same to the beans and return the pan to the oven to cook for roughly 7 minutes.
6. Mix chopped kale or mustard greens with a bit of olive oil and salt. Use clean hands to massage the seasoning into the greens. These will be used for serving.
7. Remember the mushroom marinade you saved? Scoop the tahini plus some tablespoons of water into it and stir until you get a smooth paste. To thin out the consistency, use water or balsamic vinegar. Adjust seasoning here.
8. Place cooked potatoes, beans and mushrooms on plates lined with the greens. Scoop some tahini sauce into the plate and enjoy!

Sheet Pan Breakfast Pizza With Sausage And Potatoes

- Prep time: 10 minutes
- Cooking time: 25 minutes
- Serving: 8
- Calories: 179kcal per 2 slices
- Fat: 6.9g|Protein: 14.7g|Carbs: 9.8g|Fiber: 1.3g

INGREDIENTS:

1. Unsweetened almond milk or any milk you like (½ cup)
2. Shredded potatoes (5 cups)
3. Whole egg (6 large sizes)
4. Egg yolks (6 large sizes)
5. Baby spinach (½ cup)
6. Shredded light cheddar cheese (2 tablespoons)
7. Turkey breakfast sausage like Jennie-O (16 ounces)
8. Salt
9. Black pepper powder

INSTRUCTIONS:

1. Set your oven to 375°F.
2. Grease a sheet pan (I used 10x15) with nonstick cooking spray.
3. Place the turkey sausage in a saucepan over medium heat. Use a spatula to break up the sausage while it cooks. Once it's cooked through, drain it and leave it alone.
4. Get a mixing bowl, throw in eggs, salt, spinach, pepper and milk. Mix thoroughly. Set aside.
5. Place shredded potatoes on the sheet pan and spread them out in an even layer. Layer the sausage over that and top with the spinach mixture. Use a spatula to spread it out in an even layer.
6. Sprinkle shredded cheese over the spinach mixture and slide the pan into the oven to cook for about 30 minutes or more if the eggs are not fully set.
7. Take it out of the oven and leave it to cool before slicing into 16 squares.
8. Serve warm.

Chapter Ten: Sheet Pan Vegetarian & Vegan Recipes

Baking-Sheet Pizza with Olives and Sun-Dried Tomatoes

- Prep time: 40 minutes
- Cooking time: 20 minutes
- Serving: 10
- Calories: 433 kcal
- Fat: 23g|Protein: 19g|Carbs: 42g|Fiber: 3g

INGREDIENTS:

1. Tomato sauce (1 ⅓ cups)
2. Diced provolone cheese(1 ½ cups)
3. Shredded parmesan cheese (1 cup)
4. Shredded mozzarella cheese (1 cup)
5. Oil packed sun-dried tomatoes (1 cup)
6. Pizza dough (1½ pounds)
7. Sliced red onion (½ medium size)
8. Extra virgin olive oil (⅓ cup)
9. Pitted marinated olives (1½ cups)

INSTRUCTIONS:

1. Prepare your oven. Set it to 450°F.
2. Coat a sheet pan with just 3 tablespoons of olive oil or olive oil cooking spray if you don't have enough olive oil.
3. Stretch the dough across the sheet pan carefully then use clean hands to stipple it a little bit more. Glaze the top of the dough with whatever olive oil you have left and leave it alone for roughly 20 minutes.
4. Stipple your dough a bit so it would stretch to the edge of the sheet pan. Now evenly layer tomato sauce over it.
5. Scatter shredded mozzarella, provolone and parmesan over the sauce in no particular order. Then next thing to do is carefully arrange the sun-dried tomatoes, pitted olives and red onion in a single layer over the shredded cheeses.
6. Put the sheet pan in the oven and bake for 20 minutes or extra if the cheese isn't completely melted and the crust golden brown.
7. Take the pan out of the oven and leave to cool for 10 minutes before serving.

Sheet Pan Tofu And Veggie

- Prep time: 15 minutes
- Cooking time: 30 minutes
- Serving: 4
- Calories: 360kcal
- Fat: 14g|Protein: 25g|Carbs: 40g|Fiber: 9g

INGREDIENTS:

1. Cauliflower florets (1 small head)
2. Quartered red onion wedges (1 small size)
3. Extra firm tofu (1 package)
4. Extra virgin olive oil (3 tablespoons plus 2 teaspoons)
5. Peeled carrot sliced into three quarter bits (2 medium sizes)
6. Peeled and diced sweet potatoes (1 medium size)
7. Kosher salt (1 tablespoon)
8. Asparagus with the edges trimmed and the body cut into 1-inch bits (1 small bunch)
9. Black pepper powder (1 tablespoon)

INSTRUCTIONS:

1. Prepare your oven, set it to 425°F.
2. Get a sheet pan ready, line it with parchment paper.
3. To press your tofu, place a couple of paper towels on a dinner place, set the tofu on it and cover with a couple extra paper towels. Place 4 dinner plates on top of the paper towels to put some weight on it so the moisture is expelled from the tofu.
4. Meanwhile, you have some free time so cut all your vegetables except the asparagus. Cut them into fairly large bowl. You can't add the asparagus yet because it takes very little time for it to get cooked through. You can add it close to the end of your cooking time or even halfway through.
5. Slice the tofu into 2x ½ inch rectangles and throw them into the veggie bowl. Pour exactly 2 tablespoons of olive oil into a bowl and sprinkle a quarter teaspoon of pepper and half a teaspoon of salt. Use a spatula to carefully toss the veggies and tofu until they're evenly coated with the seasoning. If it looks like it might need a bit more oil, pour in the last tablespoon.
6. Pour the tofu and veggies onto the sheet pan and spread them out in an even layer while making sure they have a bit of space in between them. If one pan clearly isn't enough, get another pan and divide the stuff.
7. Slide the pan into the oven and cook for 15 minutes.
8. Take the pan out of the oven and gently toss the tofu and veggies.
9. Tim for that asparagus you've been itching to add. Place it in a bowl and pour in 2 tablespoons of olive oil and a pinch of kosher salt. Mix thoroughly until the asparagus is properly coated in salted oil.
10. Now add it to the contents of the sheet pan(s). You're going to have to tuck it in to maintain that nice even layer you created.
11. Now return the pan to the oven and bake for about 15 minutes or until the tofu looks light brown and the vegetables are soft.
12. Take it out of the oven, adjust seasoning and serve warm.

Sheet Tray Pancakes With Peaches And Strawberries

- Prep time: 25 minutes
- Cooking time: 30 minutes
- Serving: 6
- Calories: 319kcal
- Fat: 3g|Protein: 11g|Carbs: 62g|Fiber: 3g

INGREDIENTS:

1. Salt (¼ teaspoon)
2. Nonstick cooking spray
3. Whole eggs (2 large sizes)
4. All-purpose flour (2 ½ cups)
5. Baking powder (1 tablespoon)
6. Sliced strawberries (1 ½ cups)
7. Granulated sugar (3 tablespoons)
8. Cinnamon powder (¼ teaspoon)
9. Sliced pitted peaches (2 medium sizes)
10. Buttermilk (2 cups)
11. Pure vanilla extract (½ teaspoon)
12. Maple syrup

13. Confectioners' sugar

INSTRUCTIONS:

1. Get your oven ready. Set to 425°F.
2. Prepare a sheet pan, line it with parchment paper and grease the paper with nonstick cooking spray.
3. In a medium sized mixing bowl, whisk baking powder, flour, salt, cinnamon and sugar. Stir in eggs, vanilla extract and buttermilk until you get a slightly smooth batter.
4. Spread the batter out on a baking sheet creating an even layer. Place the strawberry sliced and peaches on the top.
5. Slide the pan into the oven and bake for 15 minutes.
6. Take the pan out of the oven and sprinkle confectioners' sugar all over the top.
7. Serve in slices topped with maple syrup.

Sheet Pan Tofu Curry

- Prep time: 10 minutes
- Cooking time: 45 minutes
- Serving: 4
- Calories: 330kcal
- Fat: 23g|Protein: 19g|Carbs: 19g|Fiber: 7g

INGREDIENTS:

1. Cauliflower florets (1 head)
2. Extra virgin olive oil (¼ cup)
3. Tofu (14 oz)
4. Carrots sliced into 2 inch bits (4 medium sizes)
5. Chopped fresh parsley (¼ cup)
6. Chickpeas (1 15oz. can)
7. Garlic powder (1 teaspoon)
8. Red onions sliced into large bits (½ large size)
9. Curry spice (2 teaspoons)
10. Salt

INSTRUCTIONS:

1. Prepare your oven, set it to 375°F.
2. Pour olive oil, garlic powder, salt and curry in a small mixing bowl and mix thoroughly. Set aside.
3. In a much larger bowl, mix the veggies; carrots, cauliflower, onions and chickpeas. Drizzle the seasoning mixture over them and slowly toss to coat. Last thing on the list is tofu. Put it in the bowl and toss very gently because tofu happens to be quite fragile. Set aside.
4. Now go ahead to line your sheet pan with parchment paper which you will grease immediately after with nonstick cooking spray.
5. Pour the contents of the large mixing bowl onto the sheet pan and spread them out with a spatula.
6. Slide the pan into the oven and cook for 45 minutes. If done right, it should look golden brown and soft.
7. Serve with parsley toppings.

Sweet Potato Hash With Eggs

- Prep time: 20 minutes
- Cooking time: 30 minutes
- Serving: 4
- Calories: 353kcal
- Fat: 15g|Protein: 19g|Carbs: 32g|Fiber: 8g

INGREDIENTS:

1. Chopped onion (1 medium size)
2. Corn kernels (1 cup)
3. Parchment paper
4. Chili powder (1 ½ teaspoons)
5. Cubed sweet potatoes (2 medium sizes)
6. Chopped garlic (2 cloves)
7. Extra virgin olive oil (1 tablespoon + 1 teaspoon)
8. Chopped red bell pepper (1 medium size)
9. Cumin powder (¼ teaspoon)
10. Drained and rinsed black beans (1 cup)
11. Smoked paprika (¼ teaspoon)
12. Freshly chopped cilantro (2 tablespoons)
13. Sea or Himalayan salt (½ teaspoon)

14. Whole eggs (8 large sizes)
15. Black pepper powder (½ teaspoon)

INGREDIENTS:

1. Prepare your oven, preheat to 400°F.
2. Get a sheet pan ready, line it with parchment paper.
3. Mix onions, bell pepper, corn, sweet potato cubes, cumin, a quarter teaspoon each of salt and pepper, black beans, chili powder and paprika in a medium sized mixing bowl. Toss carefully.
4. Transfer mixture to the sheet pan. Spread it out to create an even layer.
5. Slide the pan into the oven and cook for 20 minutes. Stir with a spatula halfway through.
6. Take the pan out of the oven and make eight circles or wells in the pan.
7. Crack an egg directly into each circle then sprinkle with remaining salt and pepper.
8. Return the pan to the oven and bake for an additional 10 minutes or more if the eggs are not set.
9. Serve with cilantro toppings.

Vegan Sheet Pan Shawarma

- Prep time: 20 minutes
- Cooking time: 25 minutes
- Serving: 4
- Calories: 105g
- Fat: 5g|Protein: 5g|Carbs: 11g|Fiber: 4g

INGREDIENTS:

1. Extra virgin olive oil (½ cup)
2. Kosher salt (1 teaspoon)
3. Coriander (1 teaspoon)
4. Freshly ground black pepper (2 teaspoons)
5. Turmeric powder (1 teaspoon)
6. Cinnamon powder (½ teaspoon)
7. Fresh lemon juice (2 lemons)
8. Sweet paprika (2 teaspoons)
9. Minced garlic (6 cloves)
10. Aleppo pepper flakes (1 teaspoon)
11. Drained and rinsed chickpeas (1 can)
12. Halved lemon (1 medium size)
13. Cauliflower florets (1 large head)
14. Cubed gluten-free tempeh

15. Quartered red onions (2 small sizes)
16. Cilantro, sliced green onions or microgreens for toppings

INSTRUCTIONS:

1. Get your oven ready. Preheat to 400°F.
2. Line your sheet pan with parchment paper and set aside.
3. Mix lemon juice, pepper, garlic, cumin, olive oil, coriander, cinnamon, Aleppo pepper flakes, salt, paprika and turmeric in a medium sized mixing bowl. Mix thoroughly and pour half of the mixture in a different bowl.
4. Pour the tempeh into the first bowl. Toss to coat each bit in the mixture. Leave it alone for about 10 minutes to marinade.
5. Pour chickpeas and cauliflower florets into the other bowl. Toss with a spatula or a pair of tongs to coat. The vegetables should be evenly coated when you're done.
6. Place the tempeh on the sheet pan and top with any leftover marinade from that bowl. Next up are the chickpeas and cauliflower florets. Place these seasoned veggies all around the tempeh.
7. Place the onion quarters and lemon halves in layers with the cut side of the lemon facing down. Place one half near the bottom and the other half near the top.
8. Place the pan in the oven and cook for 30 minutes or more if the tempeh is not cooked through.
9. Take the pan out of the oven and serve on dinner plates. Squeeze the lemon halves over the veggies and tempeh. Use any toppings you like or want to try.
10. Enjoy!

Chapter Eleven: Sheet Pan Recipes For Foodies

Monkey bread

- Prep time: 30 minutes
- Cooking time:
- Serving: 8
- Calories: 1048kcal
- Fat: 194g|Protein: 15.7g|Carbs: 126.6g|Fiber: 2.3g

INGREDIENTS:

1. Kosher salt (1 pinch)
2. Biscuit dough (16 ⅓ ounce)
3. Melted unsalted butter (½
4. Cinnamon powder (2 teaspoons)
5. Sugar (½ cup)

INSTRUCTIONS:

1. Get your oven ready. Set it to 375°F.
2. Prepare your sheet pan. Line it with parchment paper then grease the paper with nonstick cooking spray.
3. Slice the biscuits in half with a very sharp knife then roll them into balls and set aside.
4. In a medium mixing bowl, pour in salt, sugar and cinnamon powder. Mix thoroughly and set aside.
5. Scoop butter into another bowl and dip each biscuit ball into the bowl to coat. Use clean hands to swirl the ball around so it's completely coated in butter.
6. Now place the coated balls in the cinnamon mixture and swirl it around until it is completely coated with it. Once you're done, place the ball on your sheet pan and repeat the process until you've gone through all the balls.
7. There'll be no need for any space in between the balls. Just pour the leftover butter on top of them and layer with the leftover cinnamon mixture.
8. Slide the pan into the oven and cook for 18 minutes. If done right, it should look puffed and baked right through the center.
9. Serve warm straight out of the pan.

Sheet Pan Sausage, Egg And Cheese Croissant Bake

- Prep time: 35 minutes
- Cooking time:
- Serving: 8
- Calories: 561.2kcal
- Fat: 37.5g|Protein: 21.4g|Carbs: 33.5g|Fiber: 1.9g

INGREDIENTS:

1. Extra virgin olive oil (1 tablespoon)
2. Sliced scallions (2 medium sizes)
3. Loose sausage (¾ lb.)
4. Whole eggs (10 large sizes)
5. Shredded parmesan or cheddar cheese (½ cup)
6. Chopped fresh parsley leaves (1/e cup)
7. Croissants that have been sliced from the top. (8 large sizes)
8. Half and half

INSTRUCTIONS:

1. Get your oven ready. Set it to 375°F.
2. Get a parchment-lined baking sheet and grease it with nonstick cooking spray. Set aside.
3. Place a medium sized saucepan over medium heat and add sausage plus olive oil. Stir for 8 minutes or more if sausage isn't completely cooked through or golden brown.
4. Turn off the heat and transfer cooked sausage to a plate.
5. Whisk eggs and half-and-half in a fairly large bowl. Do this until it looked really smooth.
6. Throw in scallions, cheese and parsley. Sprinkle a bit of pepper and salt. Whisky until everything is mixed up.
7. Use clean hands to dip the croissant halves into the egg mixture one after the other. Once a half is coated with the egg mixture, transfer it to the sheet pan. Do this until you have gone through all the halves.
8. If there is any egg mixture left, drizzle it over the croissants. Place sausage bits on top. and put the pan in the oven to cook until the eggs are set. This usually takes 20 minutes but it might take more for you because ovens are different.

Sheet Pan Taco Dutch Baby

- Prep time: 1hr 10 minutes
- Cooking time:
- Serving: 10
- Calories: 710.5kcal
- Fat: 43.9g|Protein: 31.9g|Carbs: 47.9g|Fiber: 6g

INGREDIENTS:

1. Milk (2 cups)
2. Drained chopped green chili pepper (1 can)
3. Diced bacon (12 ounces)
4. Grated cheddar cheese (1 cup)
5. Whole eggs (8 large sizes)
6. Extra virgin olive oil (2 tablespoons)
7. All-purpose flour (2 cups)
8. Grated Monterey jack cheese (1 cup)
9. Chili powder (1 teaspoon)
10. Kosher salt
11. Corn kernels (2 cups)
12. Black pepper powder
13. Thinly sliced scallions (4 medium sizes)

14. Lemon wedges
15. Diced tomatoes, cored (2 medium sizes
16. Crumbles cotija cheese (4 ounces)
17. Drained Black beans, rinsed (1 can)
18. Finely chopped cilantro (⅓ cup)
19. Hot sauce

INSTRUCTIONS:

1. Get your oven ready, set it to 425°F.
2. Spread the bacon out in an even layer on the rimmed sheet pan. Slide the pan into the oven to cook for 22 minutes. The bacos should be completely cooked through and crisp.
3. Take the bacon out of the oven and remove a third of it for toppings, leaving the rest still on the pan.
4. Pour eggs and milk into a blender and blitz until it's smooth. Add half a teaspoon of salt and flour. Blitz again until it's pasty smooth. Transfer flour mixture to the pan, right on top of the bacon. Stir with a spatula for even distribution.
5. Place cheddar, Monterrey jack and canned chilis on top and cook for 25 minutes. Just like our monkey bread, this should look puffed and browned.
6. While that is cooking, place a saucepan over medium heat and drizzle in some olive oil. Add corn and stir fry until it starts to char and look brown. This should take 5 minutes.
7. Add the beans, chili powder and seasoning (salt and pepper).
8. When the Dutch baby is all set and out of the oven, pour corn, tomatoes, black beans, cilantro, cotija cheese, scallions and bacon on top in an even layer
9. Serve with a bit of hot sauce and lime wedges.

Turkey Caprese Meatballs With Rosemary Smashed Potatoes

- Prep time: 50 minutes
- Cooking time:
- Serving: 4
- Calories: 541.6kcal
- Fat: 21.9g|Protein: 37.4g|Carbs: 34.4g|Fiber: 4.1g

INGREDIENTS:

1. Whole egg (1 large size)
2. Salt (1 teaspoon)
3. Plain breadcrumbs (½ cup)
4. Ground turkey (1lb)
5. Black pepper (1 teaspoon)
6. Cherry tomatoes (1 ½ cups)
7. Crushed red pepper flakes (¼ teaspoon)
8. Italian seasoning (1 teaspoon)
9. Shredded parmesan cheese (¼ cup)
10. Cherry tomatoes (1½ cups)
11. Chopped fresh rosemary (2 teaspoons)
12. Extra virgin olive oil (3 tablespoons)
13. Chopped fresh basil leaves (¼ cup)

14. Fresh parsley (2 tablespoons)
15. Sliced mozzarella cheese (4 ounces)
16. Small red potato (1lb.)

INSTRUCTIONS:

1. Get your oven all set, preheat to 400°F.
2. Prepare a sheet pan by lining it with parchment paper and coating the paper with cooking spray.
3. Put the turkey in a large mixing bowl. Sprinkle Italian seasoning, red pepper flakes, parsley, half a teaspoon each of salt and black pepper, breadcrumbs and parmesan then add eggs. Mix until the turkey is completely coated in seasoning.
4. Use clean hands to form balls from the mixture and place them on one end of the sheet pan. Do this until there's no ground turkey mixture left.
5. Place the tomatoes around the balls and arrange the potatoes on the other end of the baking sheet.
6. Drizzle olive oil over the balls and potatoes then sprinkle salt and pepper over the potatoes only. You already seasoned the meatballs, remember?
7. Place the pan in the oven and cook for 20 minutes or extra if the potatoes aren't smash-soft yet.
8. Use a potato masher to squash the potatoes while they're still on the pan. Add more olive oil and a sprinkle of chopped rosemary then slide the pan back into the oven and cook for an additional 10 minutes.
9. Take the pan out of the oven again and sprinkle cheese over the meatballs and tomatoes. Put the pan back into the oven but this time, to broil. Do this until the cheese is completely melted
10. Garnish with basil and serve warm.

Mixed Berry Oven Jam

- Prep time: 45 minutes
- Cooking time:
- Serving: 1
- Calories: 731kcal
- Fat: 30g|Protein: 7.7g|Carbs: 175.8g|Fiber: 29.9g

INGREDIENTS:

1. Sugar (½ cup)
2. Vanilla extract (2 teaspoons)
3. Strawberries (16 ounces)
4. Lemon zest (1 lemon)
5. Raspberries (6 ounces)
6. Salt (¼ teaspoon)
7. Blackberries (6 ounces)
8. Fresh lemon juice (2 teaspoons)

INSTRUCTIONS:

1. Prepare your oven, lads! Set it to 450°F.
2. Place enough aluminium foil inside a rimmed sheet pan then layer with parchment paper that goes up the rims of the pan. There should be no holes or your jam will leak out.
3. Hull your strawberries and slice them in half.
4. Place all the ingredients apart from the vanilla on the pan and toss gently to mix.
5. Slide the pan into the oven and bake for about 30 minutes or more if the juice isn't leaking out of the berries yet.
6. Take the pan out of the oven and finally stir in vanilla.
7. Use a fork to mash the berries still in the pan but do it gently so you don't make holes in the parchment paper. Leave it to cool for a bit.
8. Carefully pick up the sides of the parchment paper and funnel the jam into a Mason jar.
9. Use with bread or whatever you like, really.

Chapter Twelve: Sheet Pan Cookies & Dessert Recipes

Prepare your very own binge-eating worthy snack in less than 15 minutes. A plus? Your oven will do all the work while you tell me all about your day over fruit juice. What do you say?

Layered Chocolate Marshmallow Peanut Butter Brownies

- Prep time: 30 minutes
- Cooking time: 20 minutes
- Serving: 48
- Calories: 189kcal per serving
- Fat: 11g|Protein: 4g|Carbs: 21g|Fiber: 1g

INGREDIENTS:

1. Cocoa for baking (¾ cup)
2. All-purpose flour (1 ½ cups)
3. Butter (1 ½ cups)
4. Salt (½ teaspoon)
5. Whole eggs (4 large sizes)

6. Marshmallows (10 large sizes)
7. Sugar (2 cups)
8. Confectioners' sugar (2 cups)
9. Chunky peanut butter (1 jar)
10. Vanilla extract (1 teaspoon)
11. Milk (⅓ cup)

INSTRUCTIONS:

1. Get your oven ready. Preheat to 350°F.
2. Place a tiny saucepan over medium heat and melt just one cup of butter in it. Add half cocoa powder and stir until it's pasty smooth. Turn off the heat.
3. In a medium mixing bowl, mix sugar, vanilla extract and eggs thoroughly. Mix flour and salt in a different bowl and slowly stir it into the egg bowl. Now whisk in cocoa mixture.
4. Pour the contents of the bowl into a sheet pan that has already been coated with cooking spray.
5. Slide the pan into the oven and bake for about 22 minutes or until a knife inserted into the middle comes out dry. Take it out of the oven and leave to cool for a bit.
6. This step can be done while the brownies are baking or cooling. Any one works. Scoop peanut butter into a microwave safe bowl and place in the microwave to melt, not completely, just for about 30 seconds then drizzle it all over the brownies. Place brownies in the fridge for 45 minutes so the peanut butter can set.
7. While the peanut butter is busy setting, mix milk, leftover cocoa powder, marshmallows and whatever butter is left in a saucepan placed over low heat. Stir until marshmallows are melted and the mixture is fairly smooth. Turn off the heat and add confectioners' sugar. Stir until smooth.
8. Layer this over the peanut butter, refrigerate again for about 30 minutes, slice and serve.

Banana Bars with Cream Cheese Frosting

- Prep time: 15 minutes
- Cooking time: 20 minutes
- Serving: 48
- Calories: 148kcal per serving
- Fat: 7g|Protein: 1g|Carbs: 21g|Fiber: 0g

INGREDIENTS:

1. Sugar (1 ½ cups)
2. Vanilla extract (1 teaspoon)
3. Baking soda (1 teaspoon)
4. Sour cream (1 cup)
5. Melted butter (½ cup)
6. All-purpose flour (2 cups)
7. Salt (¼ teaspoon)
8. Whole eggs (2 large sizes)
9. Mashed ripe bananas (1 cup)

Frosting:

1. Melted butter (½ cup)
2. Confectioners' sugar (4 cups)
3. Melted cream cheese (1 package)
4. Vanilla extract (2 teaspoons)

INSTRUCTIONS:

1. Prepare your oven. Set to 350°F
2. Whisk butter and sugar in a large bowl until it is noticeably light and fluffy. Stir in eggs, vanilla and sour cream.
3. Mix flour, salt and baking soda in a different bowl then slowly stir it into the cream mixture. Add mashed bananas and stir until you have a thoroughly mixed batter.
4. Pour batter onto the sheet pan already coated with cooking spray. Slide the pan into the oven and bake for 25 minutes or more if you slide a toothpick in the middle and it comes out wet.
5. Take it out of the oven and leave to cool.
6. Making the frosting is generally easy. Just mix butter, vanilla and cream cheese in a bowl until it's light and fluffy.
7. Now slowly stir in confectioners' sugar until you reach the consistency of your choice. Spread all over the bars and place in the fridge.

Coconut Almond Cookie Bark

- Prep time: 25 minutes
- Cooking time: 25 minutes
- Serving: 2 pounds
- Calories: 150kcal per serving
- Fat: 9g|Protein: 2g|Carbs: 17g|Fiber: 1g

INGREDIENTS:

1. Brown sugar (½ cup)
2. All-purpose flour (2 cups)
3. Butter cubes (1 cup)
4. Almond extract (¾ teaspoon)
5. White sugar (½ cup)
6. Salt (¾ teaspoon)
7. Milk chocolate chips (1 ½ cups)
8. Whole egg (1 large size)

9. Sweetened coconut shavings(1¼ cups)
10. Sliced toasted almonds (⅓ cup)

INSTRUCTIONS:

1. Set oven to 375°F.
2. Melt butter in a saucepan set over medium heat. Stir for 8 minutes or until it looks browned. Pour melted butter into a mixing bowl and leave to cool for 15 minutes.
3. Stir in egg, white and brown sugar and vanilla extract.
4. Mix flour and salt in a different bowl and slowly fold it into sugar mixture.
5. Ads 1 cup of coconut shavings and ¾ cup of chocolate chips. Stir to spread it around the batter.
6. Pour batter onto a sheet pan and bake until it look golden brown. This took 28 minutes with my oven. Leave to cool once it's cooked through.
7. Layer the remaining coconut, almonds and chocolate chips over the cookie and place in the fridge for 15 minutes.
8. It's ready. Serve when you want.

Pistachio Brownie Toffee Bars

- Prep time: 20 minutes
- Cooking time: 30 minutes
- Serving: 36
- Calories: 219kcal per serving
- Fat: 12g|Protein: 3g|Carbs: 27g|Fiber: 1g

INGREDIENTS:

1. Brown sugar (¾ cup)
2. All-purpose flour (1½ cups)
3. Melted butter (¾ cup)
4. Egg yolk only (1 large egg)
5. Vanilla extract (¾ teaspoon)

Filling:

1. Water (⅓ cup)
2. Whole egg (1 large size)
3. Fudge brownie mix (1 package)
4. Canola oil (⅓ cup)

Topping:

1. Chopped roasted pistachios, salted (¾ cup)
2. Melted milk chocolate chips (1 package)

INSTRUCTIONS:

1. Prepare your oven. Set it to 350°F.
2. Whisk butter and brown sugar using an electric mixer. Whisk until it's fluffy.
3. Stir in egg yolk and vanilla extract.
4. Slowly stir in flour until it is thoroughly mixed.
5. Pour batter onto a greased sheet pan and slide it into the oven to cook for 14 minutes.
6. While that is baking, mix water, brownie mix, egg and oil in a bowl.
7. Take out the pan from the oven and spread filling all over the top and bake again for about 16 minutes. Leave it to cool.
8. Drizzle melted chocolate over it and top with pistachios.
9. Serve when it is completely set.

Triple Fudge Brownies

- Prep time: 10 minutes
- Cooking time: 30 minutes
- Serving: 48
- Calories: 91kcal per serving
- Fat: 9g|Protein: 1g|Carbs: 15g|Fiber: 1g

INGREDIENTS:

1. Chocolate cake mix (1 package)
2. Vanilla ice cream
3. Instant chocolate pudding mix (1 package)
4. Semi-sweet chocolate chips (2 cups)
5. Confectioners' sugar

INSTRUCTIONS:

1. Preheat your oven to 350°F.
2. You're going to have to trust the pudding manufacturer on this one. Prepare the pudding according to their directions then stir in dry chocolate cake mix and chocolate chips.
3. Pour batter onto a pan already coated with cooking spray.
4. Slide the pan into the oven and bake for 35 minutes. Sprinkle with confectioners' sugar.
5. Serve with vanilla ice cream if you'd like.

Sheet Pan Chocolate Chip Cookie Bars

- Prep time: 10 minutes
- Cooking time: 25 minutes
- Serving:24
- Calories: 314kcal
- Fat: 17g|Protein: 3g|Carbs: 40g|Fiber: 2g

INGREDIENTS:

1. Brown sugar (1¼ cups)

2. Flour (2 ¾ cups)
3. Tiny semi-sweet chocolate chips (2¼ cups)
4. Sugar (¾ cup)
5. Butter (1 cup)
6. Vanilla extract (1 tablespoon)
7. Salt (1 teaspoon)
8. Whole eggs (2 medium sizes)
9. Baking soda (1 teaspoon)

INSTRUCTIONS:

1. Prepare your oven. Set it to 350°F.
2. Mix butter, white and brown sugar in a bowl until it's light and fluffy.
3. Stir in eggs and vanilla extract.
4. Mix flour, salt and baking soda in a different bowl and slowly stir it into the cream bowl plus 2 cups of chocolate chips.
5. Grease a sheet pan and pour batter onto it.
6. Sprinkle leftover chocolate on top and slide the pan into the oven to bake for about 25 minutes. Use a toothpick to make sure the center is set.
7. Serve cool.

Peanut Butter Sheet Cake

- Prep time: 15 minutes
- Cooking time: 20 minutes
- Serving: 24
- Calories: 266kcal
- Fat: 14g|Protein: 4g|Carbs: 33g|Fiber: 1g

INGREDIENTS:

1. Baking soda (1 teaspoon)
2. Butter cubes (¾ cup)
3. All-purpose flour (2 cups)
4. Water (1 cup)
5. Chunky peanut butter (½ cup)
6. Buttermilk (½ cup)
7. Salt (½ teaspoon)
8. Sugar (2 cups)

9. Cubed butter (¾ cup)
10. Whole eggs (2 large sizes)
11. Vanilla extract (1 teaspoon)
12. Canola oil (¼ cup)

Glaze:

1. Butter (1 tablespoon)
2. Sugar (⅔ cup)
3. Mini marshmallows (⅓ cup)
4. Evaporated milk (⅓ cup)
5. Chunky peanut butter (⅓ cup)
6. Vanilla extract (½ teaspoon)

INSTRUCTIONS:

1. Get your oven ready. Set to 350°F.
2. Coat a pan with cooking spray and set aside.
3. Mix flour, baking soda, salt and sugar in a large bowl.
4. Melt butter in a saucepan then add water and leave it to boil.
5. Stir in canola oil and peanut butter until smooth.
6. Pour butter mixture into flour mixture and stir.
7. Beat eggs and mix with vanilla extract and butter milk. Stir this into the flour mixture too.
8. Pour batter onto a sheet pan and cook for 25 minutes or more if a toothpick inserted into the middle doesn't come out clean.
9. To make the glaze, mix butter, sugar and milk in a saucepan. Stir until it boils. Turn off the heat and add peanut butter, vanilla extract and marshmallows. Stir thoroughly.
10. Spread glaze over cake and serve cool.

Snickerdoodle Cookies

- Prep time: 15 minutes
- Cooking time: 10 minutes
- Serving: 35
- Calories: 140kcal
- Fat: 11g|Protein: 5g|Carbs: 9g|Fiber: 1g

Cookies:

1. Salt (½ teaspoon)

2. Unsalted butter (1 cup)
3. All-purpose flour (2 ¾ cups)
4. Cinnamon powder (1 teaspoon)
5. White sugar (1 ¼ cups)
6. Baking powder (2 teaspoons)
7. Vanilla extract (½ teaspoon)
8. Any brown sugar (¼ cup)
9. Whole eggs (2 large sizes)

Cinnamon Sugar:

1. Cinnamon powder (2 ½ teaspoons)
2. White sugar (3 tablespoons)

INGREDIENTS:

1. Prepare oven. Set it to 350°F then go ahead to line your sheet pan with parchment paper or a silicone mat.
2. Mix all the dry ingredients in a bowl and set aside.
3. Cream butter and all the sugar, white and brown using an electric mixer. Stir in vanilla extract and both eggs.
4. Reduce the speed of the mixer to low and gently whisk in dry ingredients.
5. Place plastic wrap over the bowl and put it in the fridge for 15 minutes. This makes it much easier to roll into a ball.
6. Mix cinnamon powder and white sugar. That's your cinnamon sugar, set it aside.
7. Use clean hands to roll dough into a ball, coat with cinnamon sugar and arrange on sheet pan. Do this until there isn't any dough left.
8. Put it in the oven to bake for about 10 minutes or more if it is not completely cooked through by then. The cookies should look slightly puffed when they're ready and flatten when they're cool.
9. Serve cool.

Glossary Of Equipment

1. Sheet Pan:

2. Food processor:

3. Small mixing bowl:

4. Large mixing bowl:

5. Saucepan:

6. Wooden spatula:

7. Silicone spatula:

8. Rubber spatula:

9. Parchment paper:

10. Aluminium foil:

11. Vegetable oil cooking spray:

12. Olive oil cooking spray:

13. Blender:

14. Potato masher:

Conclusion

Sharing this knowledge about the sheet pan has been fulfilling. Sheet pan recipes look and taste definitely and are most definitely not restricted to what you see in this book. There are thousands of them on the web to check out when you've exhausted my favourites over here. Sheet pan cooking accommodates all diet types, so trust me when I say there's definitely a sheet pan recipe for you.

The sheet pan cooking method is becoming increasingly popular these days and for good reason. Introduce your friends to this lifesaver and they'll spend a long long time thanking you for it. Still doubtful? Pick a recipe, give it a shot and experience the magic! Here's all the love, light, and yumminess you deserve in the world!

Made in the USA
San Bernardino, CA
28 January 2020